Jackson Pollock

by Francis V. O'Connor

The Museum of Modern Art, New York

The Museum of Modern Art is indebted to the following publishers for permission to reprint material from copyrighted articles and books:
© 1946, 1948, 1950, 1951, 1952, *Art Digest;* © 1942, 1949, 1950, 1951, 1952, 1954, *Art News;* © 1955, *Arts;* © 1944, 1954, *Arts & Architecture;* © 1945, *The Chicago Daily Tribune;* © 1948, *Life;* © 1950, *Magazine of Art;* © 1943, 1945, 1946, 1947, 1948, 1949, 1950, 1952, 1954, *The Nation;* © 1945, *The New Republic;* © 1949, 1950, 1954, *The New York Herald-Tribune;* © 1945, 1949, 1950, 1951, 1952, 1955, *The New York Times;* © 1949, *The New York World-Telegram;* © 1943, 1948, 1949, 1950, 1956, *The New Yorker;* © 1944, 1951, *Partisan Review;* © 1945, *The San Francisco Chronicle;* © 1947, 1949, 1950, 1955, *Time.* © 1951, The Devin-Adair Co., New York: *Conversations with Artists* by Selden Rodman. © 1957, Viking Press, New York: *Abstract Painting* by Thomas B. Hess.

©The Museum of Modern Art, 1967
11 West 53 Street, New York, New York 10019
Library of Congress Catalogue Card
Number 67-26814
Cover and binding design:
Joseph Bourke Del Valle
Printed in the U. S. A. by Plantin Press

Acknowledgments

Every Museum exhibition is a collaboration: of the artist, of the lenders of his works, of many friends. The current exhibition of the work of Jackson Pollock—the largest retrospective The Museum of Modern Art has ever devoted to an American artist—would have been impossible without the patience, generosity, and good will of Lee Krasner Pollock, and to her must go much of the credit for its success. I would like to express the Museum's gratitude to all the other lenders to the exhibition as well, and to thank particularly Joseph H. Hazen, who was the first lender and provided encouragement from the outset, and Mr. and Mrs. Ben Heller, Alfonso A. Ossorio, Robert U. Ossorio, and Edward F. Dragon, who gave welcome assistance at every stage.

The initial plans for the exhibition were made by the late Frank O'Hara, who was to have been its director. Following O'Hara's death—like Pollock's, a tragic accident—William S. Lieberman generously consented to take over the directorship, and brought to it his own deep knowledge and appreciation of Pollock and his work. Mr. Lieberman was assisted by many members of the Museum staff, but two require special mention: Jennifer Licht, who took much of the responsibility for research and administration pertaining to the works on canvas, and Bernice Rose, whose similar responsibility for the works on paper resulted in shedding new light on the dates of many early drawings.

Finally, I would like to thank Francis V. O'Connor, Assistant Professor of Art History at the University of Maryland, for preparing the chronological outline that forms the principal text of this catalogue, and Irene Gordon and William Berkson for the research they contributed to it.

René d'Harnoncourt

With deep gratitude I acknowledge first the generous assistance of Lee Krasner Pollock, who has given me access to her files and shared with me recollections of her late husband. I am also especially indebted to Charles Pollock and his wife Sylvia for the care and effort they expended in making available to me the Pollock family correspondence. Jackson Pollock's two other surviving brothers, Marvin Jay and Frank, and his sister-in-law, Mrs. Sanford McCoy, have been most helpful in supplying documents and photographs. The artist's teachers, Frederick Schwankovsky and, especially, Thomas Hart Benton, have helped to establish the context of Pollock's training. All these—and many others—have made their papers and recollections available to me, and have helped me in numberless ways to reconstruct Jackson Pollock's development. In due course I hope to publish a fully documented account of the artist and his career.

Preliminary research on exhibitions and criticism was provided by William Berkson. Irene Gordon performed far more than the services of an editor: pursuing innumerable details of exhibitions and their often casually recorded contents, untangling many myths and confusions, and even establishing the original identity of pictures now known by other titles (such as *Lavender Mist*) and the proper dates (as for *Blue Poles*). Finally, I want to express my appreciation to William S. Lieberman, director of the exhibition, the staff of The Museum of Modern Art Library, and the rest of the Museum staff for their generous assistance, encouragement, and patience.

Francis V. O'Connor

Number 32, 1950. Enamel on canvas, 8 feet 10 inches x 15 feet. Kunstsammlung Nordrhein-Westfalen, Düsseldorf.

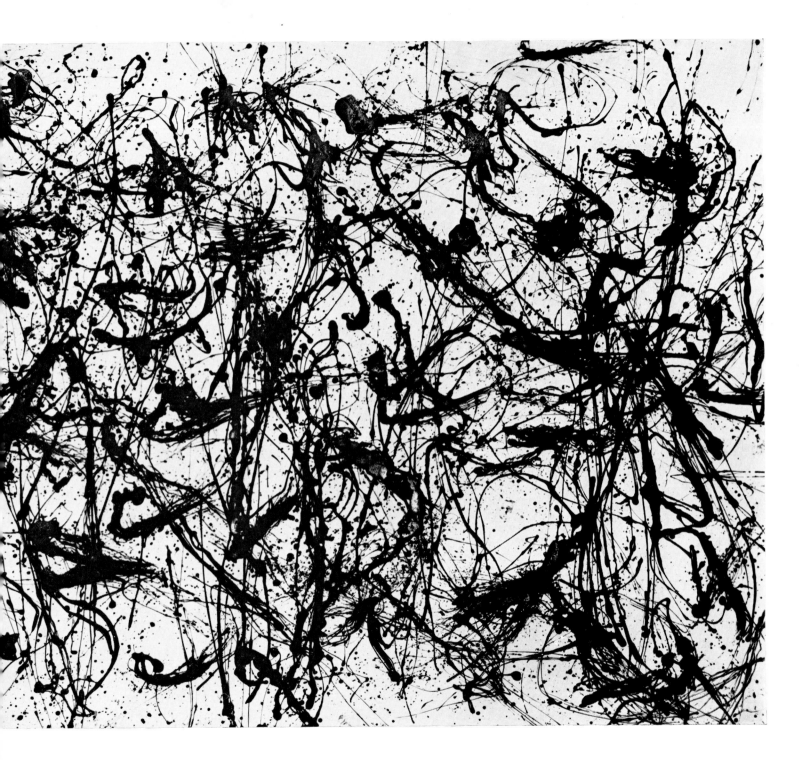

Jackson Pollock, about 1928-29

Jackson Pollock

Chronology

1912

Paul Jackson Pollock, the fifth and youngest son of Stella May McClure (1875–1958) and LeRoy Pollock (1876–1933) was born January 28 on the Watkins Ranch at Cody, Wyoming.

Both parents were of Scotch-Irish extraction (the father's original surname was McCoy before his adoption about 1890 by a family named Pollock), and both were born and raised in Tingley, Iowa. Though nominally Presbyterian, they did not raise their sons in any church. The other sons were Charles Cecil (1902–   ), Marvin Jay (1904–   ), Frank Leslie (1907–   ), and Sanford LeRoy (1909–1963). (Jackson Pollock dropped his first name—Paul—about the time he came to New York in 1930; Sanford changed his surname to McCoy sometime during the thirties.)

On Thanksgiving Day, November 28, the Pollock family left Cody for San Diego, California. Jackson never returned to the town of his birth.

1913

In August the family moved from San Diego to Phoenix, Arizona, where the father bought a truck farm of about thirty acres.

1917

The farm at Phoenix was auctioned, and the family moved to another at Chico, California. Jackson began grade school about this time. Sometime before 1922 the family moved to Janesville, California.

1922

The family moved to a farm at Orland, California. Charles, the oldest son, left home and took a job in the layout department of the *Los Angeles Times*. He studied at the Otis Art Institute through 1924. During this period he sent his brothers copies of the *Dial,* which contained many reproductions of School of Paris and other avant-garde art, and H. L. Mencken's *American Mercury*.

1923

In the autumn the family returned to Arizona to a farm outside Phoenix. Jackson was enrolled in the sixth grade of the Monroe Elementary School in Phoenix in September and remained there until February of the next year. During this period he had many opportunities to explore the old Indian ruins outside Phoenix with his brothers and friends. It was at this time, also, that the tip of his right index finger was accidentally cut off by a friend.

1924

The family moved back to Chico in the spring and later—possibly in 1925—moved to Riverside, outside Los Angeles.

1926

In September Charles registered at the Art Students League in New York City as a student of Thomas Hart Benton, who had just joined the faculty.

1927

During the summer Jackson and Sanford worked on a surveying gang along the north rim of the Grand Canyon.

In September Jackson enrolled at Riverside High School.

1928

Pollock left Riverside High School in March. In the summer the family moved into Los Angeles. In the fall Pollock enrolled at Manual Arts High School and came under the influence of an art teacher named Frederick John de St. Vrain Schwankovsky, who introduced him to Theosophy and the teachings of Krishnamurti. Since he had not been raised in any particular church, this probably constituted his first religious experience. At this time his circle of acquaintances included Philip Guston, Reuben Kadish, Manuel Tolegian, Leonard Stark, Donald Brown, and Jules Langsner.

Sometime during the academic year 1928/29 he was expelled from Manual Arts for having taken part in the publishing and distribution of two broadsides attacking the faculty and the school's overemphasis on sports.

1929

During the summer Pollock worked with his father at Santa Ynez, California. In the fall

FAR LEFT: Jackson on the farm in Arizona, about 1914

ABOVE LEFT: LeRoy Pollock, about 1925

ABOVE RIGHT: Stella Pollock with neighbor's child, Jackson in background, about 1914

BELOW: The Pollock family, Arizona, about 1914; left to right—LeRoy, Frank, Charles, Jackson, Jay, Sanford, Stella

Jackson Pollock, southern California, about 1927-28

he returned to Manual Arts, but in a letter to Charles and Frank, dated October 22, he wrote about his troubles in school, and of life and art:

I have been very busy getting adjusted in school, but another climax has arisen. I have been ousted from school again. The head of the Physical Ed. Dept. and I came to blows the other day. We saw the principal about it but he was too thick to see my side. He told me to get out and find another school. I have a number of teachers backing me so there is some possibility of my getting back. . . .

If I get back in school I will have to be very careful about my actions. The whole outfit think I am a rotten rebel from Russia. I will have to go about very quietly for a long period. . . .

I have read and re-read your letter with clearer understanding each time. Altho I am some better this year I am far from knowing the meaning of real work. I have subscribed for the "Creative Art", and "The Arts". From the Creative Art I am able to under stand you better and it gives me a new outlook on life.

I have dropped religion for the present. Should I follow the Occult Mysticism it wouldn't be for commercial purposes. I am doubtful of any talent, so what ever I choose to be, will be accomplished only by long study and work. I fear it will be forced and mechanical. Architecture interests me but not in the sense painting and sculptoring does. I became acquainted with Rivera's work through a number of Communist meetings I attended after being ousted from school last year. He has a painting in the Museum now. Perhaps you have seen it, Dia de Flores. I found the Creative Art January 1929 on Rivera. I certainly admire his work. The other magazines I could not find.

As to what I would like to be. It is difficult to say. An Artist of some kind. If nothing else I shall always study the Arts. People have always frightened and bored me consequently I have been within my own shell and have not accomplished anything materially. In fact to talk in a group I was so frightened that I could not think logically. I am gradually overcoming it now. I am taking American Literature, Contemporary Literature, Clay Modeling and the life class. We are very fortunate in that this is the only school in the city that have models. Altho it is difficult to have a nude and get by the board, Schwankavsky is brave enough to have them.

1930

With the help of Schwankovsky, Pollock was permitted to enroll again at Manual Arts for the spring term, but on a part-time basis. He took classes in clay modeling and life drawing half the day and worked and read at home the other half. He found this an agreeable arrangement. Writing to Charles in New York on January 31, he said:

i am continually having new experiences and am going through a wavering evolution which leave my mind in an unsettled state. too i am a bit lazy and careless with my correspondance i am sorry i seem so uninterested in your helping me but from now on there will be more interest and a hastier reply to your letters. my letters are undoubtedly egotistical but it is myself that i am interested in now. i suppose mother keeps you posted on family matter

school is still boresome but i have settled myself to its rules and the ringing bells so i have not been in trouble lately. this term i am going to go but one half day the rest i will spend reading and working here at home. i am quite sure i will be able to accomplish a lot more. in school i will take life drawing and clay modeling. i have started doing some thing with clay and have found a bit of encouragement from my teacher. my drawing i will tell you frankly is rotten it seems to lack freedom and rythem it is cold and lifeless. it isn't worth the postage to send it. i think there should be an advancement soon if it is ever to come and then i will send you some drawings. the truth of it is i have never really gotten down to real work and finish a piece i usually get disgusted with it and lose interest. water color i like but have never worked with it much. altho i feel i will make an artist of some kind i have never proven to myself nor any body else that i have it in me.

this

so called happy part of one's life youth to me is a bit of damnable hell if i could come to some conclusion about my self and life perhaps then i could see something to work for. my mind blazes up with some illusion for a couple of weeks then it smoalters down to a bit of nothing the more i read and the more i think i am thinking the darker things become. i am still interested in theosophy and am studying a book light on the path every thing it has to say seems to be contrary to the essence of modern life but after it is understood and lived up to i think it is a very helpful guide. i wish you would get one and tell me what you think of it. they only cost thirty cents if you can not find one i will send you one.

we have

gotten up a group and have arranged for a furnace where we can have our stuff fired. we will give the owner a commission for the firing and glazing. there is chance of my making a little book money.

i am

hoping you will flow freely with criticism and advice and book lists i no longer dream as i used to perhaps i can derive some good from it.

In June Charles and Frank, who was studying literature at Columbia University, returned to Los Angeles for the summer. The same month Jackson and Charles went to Pomona College to see José Clemente Orozco's newly completed fresco, *Prometheus*.

In the fall Jackson accompanied Charles and Frank to New York City with the idea of studying art there. On September 29 Jackson registered at the Art Students League in Thomas Hart Benton's class, Life Drawing, Painting, and Composition, which met five evenings a week, from 7:00 to 10:00 P.M., with the instructor giving criticisms twice a week; the tuition was $12.00 a month. Pollock gave his address as 240 West 14th Street.

In October Benton and Orozco began murals at The New School for Social Research. Their work continued through the winter. Pollock did "action posing" for Benton and probably met Orozco at this time.

1931

In February Pollock was granted student aid, and re-entered Benton's class in which he continued through May. In June Charles married Elizabeth England. Early the same month Pollock and Manuel Tolegian, a friend from Los Angeles who was also a student of Benton's, started out together to hitchhike home across the country. Following the example of their teacher, they intended to devote the trip to sketching "local color." In July, having arrived in Los Angeles, Jackson reported his experience to Charles:

> My trip was a peach. I got a number of kicks in the but and put in jail twice with days of hunger—but what a worthwhile experience. I would be on the road yet if my money had lasted. I got in Monday afternoon exactly three weeks after starting. The country began getting interesting in Kansas—the wheat was just beginning to turn and the farmers were making preparation for harvest. I saw the negroes playing poker, shooting craps and dancing along the Mississippi in St. Louis. The miners and prostitutes in Terre Haute Indiana gave swell color—their both starving—working for a quarter—digging their graves.
>
> I quit the highway in southern Kansas and grabbed a freight—went through Oklahoma and the Panhandle of Texas—met a lot of interesting bums—cut throats and the average American looking for work—the freights are full, men going west men going east and as many going north and south a million of them. I rode trains through to San Bernardino and caught a ride into Los Angeles. Tolegian made the trip in 11 days he got a thru ride from Pueblo to L.A. I guess he had a fine trip—neither of us did much drawing.

During the summer Pollock worked as a lumberjack at Big Pines, California. As fall approached he began to think of the future and wrote to Charles:

Jackson Pollock, about 1930

The folks have probably told you that I have been cutting wood—I have finished up the job today—and after figuring things out there is damned little left—barely enough to pay for my salt—at any rate I'm built up again and feel fine. I wish you and Frank could have gotten out for the summer—its quite a relief. I guess the short stay in the country helped. I haven't done any drawing to speak of. Some more study with Benton and a lot of work is lacking—the old bunch out here are quite haywire—they think worse of me tho. . . .

I don't know what to try and do—more and more I realize I'm sadly in need of some method of making a living—and its beginning to look as tho I'll have to take time off if I'm ever to get started. To make matters worse, I haven't any particular interest in that kind of stuff. There is little difficulty in getting back there—and I suppose I can find something to do—what is your opinion? The trip through the country is worthwhile regardless of how I might have to make it. I landed here with a dime but could have made the trip easily on ten dollars. . . .

Dad still has difficulties in losing money—and thinks I'm just a bum—while mother still holds the old love.

Pollock decided to return to New York and on October 12, after another adventurous cross-country trip, registered at the League on a tuition loan in Benton's class in mural painting. It met six mornings a week from 9:00 A.M. to 12:30 P.M., with two criticisms. He gave his address as 49 East 10th Street.

1932

In May Pollock ended his second year at the League. During the summer he made another sketching trip, this time with Whitney Darrow, Jr., a friend from the League, traveling west via southern Canada and Detroit. They spent the summer in Los Angeles and went once to see David Alfaro Siqueiros' exterior murals at the Chouinard Art School. In the fall Darrow bought an old Ford, and they returned to the East via New Orleans.

Pollock registered at the League on October 3 and again took Benton's mural painting class, which continued to meet at the same time in the morning. He was appointed monitor of the class and was thus exempted from paying tuition. He gave his address as 46 Carmine Street.

In December Benton left the League to take a major mural commission offered by the State of Indiana. The same month Pollock became a member of the League. This membership (which he let expire in December 1935) allowed him to use the graphic arts studio on

Saturdays. Although Pollock made lithographs on occasion throughout the thirties, it is not clear whether he took advantage of the League's facilities immediately. After about 1934, however, he usually relied on the technical assistance of the printmaker, Theodore Wahl, who pulled many of his editions.

1933

Benton having gone, Pollock registered for January in John Sloan's class, Life Drawing, Painting, and Composition. The same month he learned that his father was incurably ill.

For February and March Pollock registered in Robert Laurent's sculpture class.

On March 6 LeRoy Pollock died in Los Angeles of malignant endocarditis. Jackson, Charles, and Frank were too poor to go to Los Angeles for the funeral. Shortly afterward, Jackson, along with Charles and his wife Elizabeth, moved into an apartment at 46 East 8th Street. Charles was employed teaching one day a week at the City and Country School and had occasional free-lance commercial art jobs.

During the summer Pollock watched Diego Rivera paint murals on movable wall panels at the New Workers' School on West 14th Street.

In the autumn Benton returned to New York and the League. Pollock did not resume studying with him but took part in Benton's musical Monday evenings with Manuel Tolegian, Joseph Meert, Beauford Delaney, and Bernard Steffan, among others. Pollock continued to attend these through the spring of 1935, when Benton went to Kansas City to stay. He did not, however, lose all contact with his teacher; through 1937 Pollock regularly spent a few weeks each summer with the Bentons at their home in Chilmark on Martha's Vineyard, and some of Pollock's early paintings depict Vineyard scenes. Benton was a constant source of encouragement to the young man. In an undated letter, which can be placed sometime before the spring of 1935, Benton wrote:

> Before I get started on my own stuff and forget everything else I want to tell you I think the little sketches you left around here are magnificent. Your color is rich and beautiful. You've the stuff old kid—all you have to do is keep it up. You ought to give some time to drawing—but I do not somehow or other feel the lack of drawing in the stuff left here. It seems to *go* without it. Rita has framed your little lithograph and it carries well. See you around the tenth with the others.

1934

During the winter of 1933/34 Pollock produced a number of small, experimental works.

LEFT: The Pollock family, 1917; back row, left to right—Charles, Stella, Jay; front row, left to right—Sanford, LeRoy, Frank, Jackson

RIGHT: *Woman.* (1934?). Oil on gesso ground on composition board, $14\frac{1}{8}$ x $10\frac{5}{8}$ inches. Estate of the artist

Among these were two mural sketches for lunettes at Greenwich House, which were never executed.

That summer Jackson and Charles took an 8,000 mile journey in a 1926 Model T Ford. They visited the coal mining regions of Pennsylvania, West Virginia, and Harlan County, Kentucky, and then traveled to California through Tennessee, Mississippi, Louisiana, Texas, New Mexico, and Arizona. In Los Angeles they visited their widowed mother and made occasional camping trips into the Mojave Desert and other places. On the return trip east they stopped off at Tingley, Iowa, to visit their mother's sister on her farm and were horrified at the abject poverty they found there due to the Depression.

On his return to New York Pollock moved to a small apartment at 76 West Houston Street. In October Sanford joined him in New York. Both found employment as janitors at the City and Country School. It was probably at this time that Caroline Pratt, the director of the school, and Helen Marot, a teacher there who was deeply interested in psychology, came to know Jackson. Both women took an interest in the troubled young man and were to be sources of encouragement and help to him throughout the thirties.

About this time Jackson and Sanford, who were both on relief, would occasionally steal fuel and food from pushcarts. In Washington Square they were struck by the contrast of men huddling in the dark shadows of a New York University building while the lights in the windows above illuminated the masterpieces of the A. E. Gallatin Collection. Both brothers painted works depicting the scene, which were later exhibited at the John Reed Club.

In December Benton's wife Rita was instrumental in organizing a sales exhibition in the basement of the Ferargil Gallery, operated by Frederic Newlin Price, who handled her husband's works. Pollock helped organize the exhibition and run the sales. With the assistance of the Bentons he painted a number of ceramic plates and bowls, which were sold through the exhibition. Mrs. Benton maintained this outlet for indigent artists through the late spring of 1935.

1935

Pollock showed a work called *Threshers* in the EIGHTH EXHIBITION OF WATERCOLORS, PASTELS, AND DRAWINGS BY AMERICAN AND FRENCH ARTISTS, held at the Brooklyn Museum, February 1–28. He gave his gallery as the Ferargil, though he was never to have a formal contract with Frederic Price.

On February 25 Pollock was employed as a "stonecutter" by the New York City Emergency Relief Bureau to restore public monuments at $1.75 an hour. He was later made a "stonecutter's assistant" at eighty-five cents an hour. He worked through July cleaning Augustus Saint-Gaudens' statue of Peter Cooper in Cooper Square.

On August 1 Pollock signed up with the newly created Federal Art Project of the Works Progress Administration (WPA). He joined the easel division at an initial salary of $103.40 per month, which was changed to $95.44 per four-week fiscal period. He was required to submit for allocation one painting about every eight weeks, depending on its size and his normal rate of production. This he did, with several interruptions, until the end of the Project early in 1943. The resulting financial security (such as it was—his total wages for the eight-year period amounted to about $7,800) permitted him to experiment freely, developing a personal style that became more apparent after 1938.

In September Charles went to Washington, D.C., to work with the Resettlement Administration. Hereafter he would have only limited contact with his youngest brother. Sanford and Jackson moved into the apartment at 46 East 8th Street, which was to remain Pollock's home and studio until he moved to East Hampton in 1945. Sanford was to play a most important role in Pollock's life. He made many sacrifices to help his troubled younger brother, often to the detriment of his own artistic career.

David Alfaro Siqueiros and Jackson Pollock, New York, 1936

1936

Early in the year Sanford married Arloie Conaway, a girl he first met in Los Angeles.

In the spring Siqueiros established an "experimental workshop" at 5 West 14th Street, on the west side of Union Square, in which Sanford and Jackson worked. Siqueiros was engaged in exploring new techniques and mediums applicable to mural painting as well as to the banners and floats he frequently produced for Communist demonstrations. Among the many experiments was the use of spray guns and air brushes along with the latest synthetic paints and lacquers, including Duco. The spontaneous application of paint and the problems of "controlled accidents" occupied the members of the workshop. The floor was covered with spatter and drip. It is likely that this experience had an influence on Pollock's later development.

In the fall Pollock left the city for a few weeks and took a house near Frenchtown, New Jersey. During this time he wrecked in an accident a car that Charles had signed over to him earlier in the year.

Pollock worked on the Federal Art Project all year. In November, government records indicate, two works that Pollock had given to the Project were allocated. One, a gouache, was called *White Horse Grazing;* the other, an oil, was titled *Construction.* It is not known whether these works still exist. Of the fifty-odd paintings Pollock submitted for allocation between 1935 and 1943, only two are known to be extant.

During this same year Jackson met Lenore ("Lee") Krasner briefly at a loft party; they were not to meet again until late in 1941.

1937

Sometime in January Pollock began psychiatric treatment for alcoholism.

In February he exhibited a tempera painting titled *Cotton Pickers* at the Temporary Galleries of the Municipal Art Committee, 62 West 53rd Street, New York City. These galleries, under the direction of Marchal E. Landgren, provided free exhibition space to self-organized groups of artists working in the city; the exhibited work remained the property of the artist and was offered for sale without commission charged by the Committee. Sanford, Philip Guston, Bernard Steffan, and Manuel Tolegian, among others, showed in the same group.

Charles moved to Detroit to take a job as a layout editor and political cartoonist for the United Automobile Workers.

It is possible that Pollock first met the artist-critic John Graham about this time after reading his article, "Primitive Art and Picasso," in the April issue of the *Magazine of Art*. Graham, who became an important influence on Pollock in the late thirties, was impressed with Pollock's work and intended to add his name to his list of promising young American artists in the second edition of his *System and Dialectics of Art*.

On July 21 Pollock was arrested at Martha's Vineyard for drunkenness and disturbing the peace. Benton, whom he was visiting, paid the $10 fine. On July 27 Sanford wrote to Charles and explained why he could not come to Detroit to take a job with the United Automobile Workers newspaper:

> Jack has been having a very difficult time with himself. This past year has been a succession of periods of emotional instability for him which is usually expressed by a complete loss of responsibility both to himself and to us. Accompanied, of course, with drinking. It came to the point where it was obvious that the man needed help. He was mentally sick. So I took him to a well recommended Doctor, a Psychiatrist, who has been trying to help the man find himself. As you know troubles such as his are very deep-rooted, in childhood usually, and it takes a long while to get them ironed out. He has been going some six months now and I feel there is a slight improvement in his point of view. So without giving the impression that I am trying to be a wet nurse to Jack, honestly I would be fearful of the results if he were left alone with no one to keep him in check. . . . There is no cause for alarm, he simply must be watched and guided intelligently. . . . Jack is at the Vineyard for a three week vacation. I am sure it will do him much good.

In September Sanford closed off the front room of the 8th Street apartment so that Jackson could have a private studio. In the hard years to come it would occasionally be necessary to rent this room to friends.

In October Pollock exhibited a watercolor in the opening show at the new WPA Federal Art Gallery at 225 West 57th Street.

Early in December Benton came to New York and invited Jackson and Sanford to spend Christmas in Kansas City. Sanford could not leave the Project, but Jackson got permission and traveled by bus to Missouri. (Aside from some brief encounters in New York City in the early 1940s, this was the last time Pollock spent any time in the company of his teacher. In later years, however, right up through the year of his death, he would occasionally telephone Benton in Kansas City.)

1938

Early in January on his way back to New York from Missouri Jackson visited Charles in Detroit.

In February Sanford wrote to Charles:

> Our plans for the summer are very indefinite except for one important thing which is to get Jack out of New York. It has only been with a very commendable and courageous effort on his part that he has held himself in check. I don't remember whether I told you but in the first part of the winter he was in serious mental shape and I was worried as hell about him. He's in pretty good condition now, doing some fine work but needs relief badly from New York.

By mid-May Pollock had made definite plans to accompany Benton on a six-week sketching trip, but was unable to do so because the Project would not give him another leave of absence. On June 9, his records show, his employment was terminated because of "continued absence." On June 11, at his own request and with the assistance of his psychiatrist and Helen Marot, Pollock entered the Westchester Division of New York Hospital for treatment of acute alcoholism. He remained there until September; during the period of his therapy he made a number of hammered copper bowls and plaques.

On October 3 the Bentons wrote him from Kansas City:

> I saw your stuff in N.Y. and later a picture that my brother has. I am very strongly for you as an artist. You're a damn fool if you don't cut out the monkey business and get to work.
>
> Tom
>
> I was worried about you for 4 months, and can't tell you how relieved I was to hear from you.
> We all hope & pray that you settle down & work—& we mean *work hard paint hard*— So few have the ability to say something interesting thru their work—You have— Tom & I & many others believe in you. . . .
> Tom gave up drinking last July and this summer he had a most productive one and greatly improved. . . .
> Do let us hear from you. Remember our house is always opened for you. . . .
>
> Rita

On November 23 Pollock was reassigned to the easel division of the Project, though his wage was reduced to $91.00 per four-week fiscal period.

1939

Early in the year Pollock re-entered psychoanalysis, which continued through the summer of 1940. His doctor, a Jungian, used his drawings as a therapeutic aid.

Because of pressure on the WPA from Congress and other sources, many artists were laid off the Project, thus increasing the burden of anxiety on the Pollock household. Sanford wrote to Charles in March:

> We have been investigated on the project. Don't know yet what the result of it will be. Should they ever catch up with my pack of lies they'll probably put us in jail and throw the key away! They are mighty clever at keeping the employees in a constant state of jitters. Jack is still struggling with the problems of painting and living.

Jackson and Sanford rented a place in Bucks County, Pennsylvania, for the summer. In July the Federal Art Project was reorganized as the WPA Art Program. Under one of the new provisions enacted by Congress all artists employed for more than eighteen months were fired. Sanford was laid off in August under this clause, but had himself recertified for relief and was re-employed by December.

1940

In May Sanford wrote to Charles:

> Jack is doing very good work. After years of trying to work along lines completely unsympathetic to his nature, he has finally dropped the Benton nonsense and is coming out with an honest creative art.

On May 22 Pollock was fired from the Project under the eighteen-month clause. Early in June Sanford wrote to Charles:

> We on the project have been forced to sign an affidavit to the effect that we belonged to neither the Communist or Nazi parties. A wholly illegal procedure. And now I understand the army is snooping around the Project finding out how the artists could fit into the "Defense Program".
>
> Jack is still off the Project. It would be necessary for him to get on relief before he could get his job back. And the relief bureau is making it as miserable as possible for single men. Trying such tricks as suggesting that the Army has openings for healthy young men. . . . I would just as soon that Jack don't get tangled up in the Relief mess and instead have a good healthy summer in the country. It makes any one nervous to have to go through such an humiliating experience and Jack is especially sensitive to that sort of nasty business.

That summer Jackson wrote to Charles:

> I haven't much to say about my work and things—only that I have been going through

violent changes the past couple of years. God knows what will come out of it all—it's pretty negative stuff so far. . . . I haven't been up to any of those competitions. Will try when my work clears up a little more. Phil Guston and his wife have been winning some of the smaller jobs. I'm still trying to get back on the project and it doesn't look any too damned good. At best it will be another four or five weeks, and then it may be the army instead.

Pollock managed to get back on the Project by October 10. On October 16 he registered for the draft with Local Board No. 17. On October 22 Sanford again described to Charles the tension under which they were living:

> They are dropping people like flies on the pretense that they are Reds, for having signed a petition about a year ago to have the C.P. put on the ballot. We remember signing it so we are nervously awaiting the axe. They got 20 in my department in one day last week. There is no redress. The irony of it is that the real Party People I know didn't sign the damn thing and it is suckers like us who are getting it. I could kick myself in the ass for being a damn fool—but who would of thought they could ever pull one as raw as that. Further more, when they get us in the Army with the notion that we are Reds you can bet they will burn our hides. Needless to say we are rigid with fright.

1941

In April Pollock was classified for the draft as IV-F. At this time he was in treatment with another Jungian analyst who also utilized his drawings during the sessions.

In July Sanford provided an insight into Jackson's artistic development in a letter to Charles:

> Jackson's art . . . if he allows [it] to grow, will, I am convinced, come to great importance. As I have inferred in other letters, he has thrown off the yoke of Benton completely and is doing work which is creative in the most genuine sense of the word. Here again, although I "feel" its meaning and implication, I am not qualified to present it in terms of words. His thinking is, I think, related to that of men like Beckmann, Orozco and Picasso. We are sure that if he is able to hold himself together his work will become of real significance. His painting is abstract, intense, evocative in quality.

In November John Graham invited Pollock to exhibit in a show he was organizing at the McMillen gallery. Lee Krasner—recently a student of Hans Hofmann—was invited also. When she learned that Pollock lived just around the corner from her, she visited him, thus beginning a relationship that was to last until his death.

up the difference. She also scheduled a one-man show for Pollock in November and commissioned a mural-sized painting for the entrance hall of her 61st Street town house. This patronage enabled Pollock to quit his custodial job at the museum in midsummer and to return to full-time painting.

In a card to Lee Krasner postmarked July 15, he wrote:

> Have signed the contract and have seen the wall space for the mural—it's all very exciting.

In a letter dated July 29 he described his situation to Charles:

> Things really broke with the showing of that painting [*Stenographic Figure*]. I had a pretty good mention in the *Nation*—I have a year's contract with The Art of This Century and a large painting to do for Peggy Guggenheim's house, 8′11 ½″ x 19′9″. With no strings as to what or how I paint it. I am going to paint it in oil on canvas. They are giving me a show Nov. 16 and I want to have the painting finished for the show. I've had to tear out the partition between the front and middle room to get the damned thing up. I have it stretched now. It looks pretty big, but exciting as all hell.

From August Pollock worked on a number of smaller paintings for his November show. Some cards from Howard Putzel indicate the progress toward the show; one postmarked October 2:

> Haven't had a minute since your pictures arrived with the Chiricos. The small painting, "Conflict" didn't come. Hope you'll bring it.
>
> Soby dropped in this afternoon and is mad about your work. Not up the alley of his collection, but he says the Modern Museum should buy "The She-Wolf", and also predicts you'll be THE new sensation of this season, and, moreover, that, unlike past season's sensations, that you'll last.
>
> Hope you and Lee will come to the preview of the Chirico: Monday from 4 to 6. Really a superb show.
>
> Hope you're producing some small pictures for poor people. Best to Lee.

Another postmarked November 1:

> I just reserved three tickets for Segovia for Wednesday (our date). If you detest Segovia, please notify me pronto. Just thought: we should have the new pictures for photos. How about taxi-ing them up here Wednesday 5:30 to 6 (gallery expense). . . .
>
> HP
>
> P.S. Lee, if you have time Tuesday can (or will) you help fold 1200 catalogues?

Stenographic Figure. (1942). Oil on canvas, 40 x 55¾ inches. Estate of the artist

Peggy Guggenheim and Jackson Pollock in front of the mural he painted for the hallway of her home, 1946 (see pages 90–91)

About this time Pollock began treatment with a homeopathic physician in New York, with whom he would consult more or less regularly until his death.

After the November show at Art of This Century closed Pollock turned again to Miss Guggenheim's mural. He sat for hours in front of the huge—and as yet untouched—canvas. Finally, sometime in December, or possibly during the first weeks of January, he painted the entire work in a single session of frenzied creativity.

April 16–May 15. Art of This Century, New York. EXHIBITION OF COLLAGE. 1 work.

> JEAN CONNOLLY (*Nation*, May 1)
> There are some fine examples by [Picasso] here, and also some nice ones by Baziotes, Pollock and Reinhardt.

May 18–June 26. Art of This Century, New York. SPRING SALON FOR YOUNG ARTISTS. 1 painting: *Stenographic Figure*. The jury consisted of Alfred H. Barr, Jr., Marcel Duchamp, Jimmy Ernst, Max Ernst, Piet Mondrian, James Thrall Soby, and James Johnson Sweeney, with Peggy Guggenheim and Howard Putzel representing the gallery.

> JEAN CONNOLLY (*Nation*, May 29)
> This is a show of artists under thirty-five years old. It is a good one, and for once the future reveals a gleam of hope . . . there is a large painting by Jackson Pollock which, I am told, made the jury starry-eyed.

> ROBERT M. COATES (*New Yorker*, May 29)
> Despite a faint air of the haphazard about the hanging and a certain amount of deadwood in the paintings, the new show at Art of This Century . . . deserves your attention. A jury affair, it is the first of its sort that I have known to devote itself strictly to those twin branches of advanced modern painting, abstractionism and surrealism, and as such it has attracted a lot of new talent; to most people . . . at least two-thirds of the thirty-odd artists represented will be totally unknown. A good share of the work is amateurish. . . . But in Jackson Pollock's abstract "Painting," with its curious reminiscences of both Matisse and Miró, we have a real discovery.

pp. 86-88

November 9–27. Art of This Century, New York. One-man show. The catalogue listed the following works: *Male and Female, The Guardians of the Secret, The She-Wolf, The Moon-Woman, The Moon-Woman Cuts the Circle, The Mad Moon-Woman, Stenographic Figure, Conflict, The Magic Mirror,* 6 Untitled, plus gouaches and drawings. It is not clear whether two paintings were added to the show—*Male and Female in Search for a Symbol* (title later changed to *Search for a Symbol*) and *Wounded Animal*—or whether these titles were given to paintings listed as Untitled. The catalogue essay by James Johnson Sweeney was the first critical evaluation of Pollock:

p. 31

"Talent, will, genius," as George Sand wrote Flaubert, "are natural phenomena like the lake, the volcano, the mountain, the wind, the star, the cloud." Pollock's talent is volcanic. It has fire. It is unpredictable. It is undisciplined. It spills itself out in a mineral prodigality not yet crystalized. It is lavish, explosive, untidy.

But young painters, particularly Americans, tend to be too careful of opinion. Too often the dish is allowed to chill in the serving. What we need is more young men who paint from inner impulsion without an ear to what the critic or spectator may feel— painters who will risk spoiling a canvas to say something in their own way. Pollock is one.

It is true that Pollock needs self-discipline. But to profit from pruning, a plant must have vitality. In art we are only too familiar with the application of self-discipline where liberation would have been more profitable. Pollock can stand it. In his early work as a student of Thomas Benton he showed a conventional academic competence. Today his creed is evidently that of Hugo, "Ballast yourself with reality and throw yourself into the sea. The sea is inspiration."

Among young painters, Jackson Pollock offers unusual promise in his exuberance, independence, and native sensibility. If he continues to exploit these qualities with the courage and conscience he has shown so far, he will fulfill that promise.

EDWARD ALDEN JEWELL (*New York Times,* November 14)
These cannot be called nonobjective abstractions, for most of them have fairly naturalistic titles, and two that are marked "Untitled" have become particularized by the artist since the catalogue went to press. What looks slightly like a dog begging turns out instead to be "Wounded Animal." The most recent canvas, a scattered design against pink, represents "Male and Female in Search of a Symbol." . . .

Most of the abstractions are large and nearly all of them are extravagantly, not to say savagely, romantic. Here is obscurantism indeed, though it may become resolved and clarified as the artist proceeds. This is his first one-man show.

ROBERT M. COATES (*New Yorker,* November 20)
At Art of This Century there is what seems to be an authentic discovery—the paintings of Jackson Pollock, a young Western artist who is having his first one-man exhibition there. Mr. Pollock's style, which is a curious mixture of the abstract and the symbolic, is almost wholly individual, and the effect of his one noticeable influence, Picasso, is a healthy one, for it imposes a certain symmetry on his work without detracting from its basic force and vigor. Sometimes, as in "Stenographic Figure" and "The She-Wolf," Mr. Pollock's forcefulness, coupled with a persistent tendency to overwork his ideas, leads him into turgidity. But his color is always rich and daring, his approach mature, and his design remarkably fluent, and I had the satisfied feeling that in such pieces as "The Magic Mirror" and "The Wounded Animal" he had succeeded pretty well and pretty clearly in achieving just what he was aiming at.

CLEMENT GREENBERG (*Nation,* November 27)
There are both surprise and fulfillment in Jackson Pollock's not so abstract abstractions. He is the

first painter I know of to have got something positive from the muddiness of color that so profoundly characterizes a great deal of American painting. It is the equivalent, even if in a negative, helpless way, of that American chiaroscuro which dominated Melville, Hawthorne, Poe, and has been best translated into painting by Blakelock and Ryder. The mud abounds in Pollock's larger works, and these, though the least consummated, are his most original and ambitious. Being young and full of energy, he takes orders he can't fill. In the large, audacious "Guardians of the Secret" he struggles between two slabs of inscribed mud (Pollock almost always *inscribes* his purer colors); and space tautens but does not burst into a picture; nor is the mud quite transmuted. Both this painting and "Male and Female" (Pollock's titles are pretentious) zigzags between the intensity of the easel picture and the blandness of the mural. The smaller works are much more conclusive: the smallest one of all, "Conflict," and "Wounded Animal," with its chalky incrustation, are among the strongest abstract paintings I have yet seen by an American. Here Pollock's force has just the right amount of space to expand in; whereas in larger format he spends himself in too many directions at once. Pollock has gone through the influences of Miró, Picasso, Mexican painting, and what not, and has come out on the other side at the age of thirty-one, painting mostly with his own brush. In his search for style he is liable to relapse into an influence, but if the times are propitious, it won't be for long.

ROBERT MOTHERWELL (*Partisan Review*, Winter 1944)
[Pollock] represents one of the younger generation's chances. There are not three other painters of whom this could be said. In his exhibit, Pollock reveals extraordinary gifts: his color sense is remarkably fine, never exploited beyond its proper role; and his sense of surface is equally good. His principal problem is to discover what his true subject is. And since painting is his thought's medium, the resolution must grow out of the process of his painting itself.

November 30 [?]–December 31. Art of This Century, New York. NATURAL, INSANE, SURREALIST ART. 1 drawing: Untitled (1943). Examples of the art of the insane, the art of nature, and the art of the Surrealists were exhibited together. The art of nature included twisted driftwood, petrified tree roots, jaw bones with teeth. Among the Surrealists' works were stabiles by Alexander Calder, and gouaches, drawings, and watercolors by Joseph Cornell, Max Ernst, André Masson, Matta, Miró, Motherwell, and Yves Tanguy.

1944

The February issue of *Arts & Architecture* carried the following questionnaire, which, Lee Pollock recalls, was formulated by Pollock with the assistance of Howard Putzel:

Where were you born?
Cody, Wyoming, in January, 1912. My ancestors were Scotch and Irish.

Have you traveled any?
I've knocked around some in California, some in Arizona. Never been to Europe.

Wounded Animal. 1943. Oil and plaster on canvas, 38 x 30 inches. Collection Thomas B. Hess, New York

Would you like to go abroad?

No. I don't see why the problems of modern painting can't be solved as well here as elsewhere.

Where did you study?

At the Art Student's League, here in New York. I began when I was seventeen. Studied with Benton, at the League, for two years.

How did your study with Thomas Benton affect your work, which differs so radically from his?

My work with Benton was important as something against which to react very strongly, later on; in this, it was better to have worked with him than with a less resistant personality who would have provided a much less strong opposition. At the same time, Benton introduced me to Renaissance art.

Why do you prefer living here in New York to your native West?

Living is keener, more demanding, more intense and expansive in New York than in the West; the stimulating influences are more numerous and rewarding. At the same time, I have a definite feeling for the West: the vast horizontality of the land, for instance; here only the Atlantic ocean gives you that.

Has being a Westerner affected your work?

I have always been very impressed with the plastic qualities of American Indian art. The Indians have the true painter's approach in their capacity to get hold of appropriate images, and in their understanding of what constitutes painterly subject-matter. Their color is essentially Western, their vision has the basic universality of all real art. Some people find references to American Indian art and calligraphy in parts of my pictures. That wasn't intentional; probably was the result of early memories and enthusiasms.

Do you consider technique to be important in art?

Yes and no. Craftsmanship is essential to the artist. He needs it just as he needs brushes, pigments, and a surface to paint on.

Do you find it important that many famous modern European artists are living in this country?

Yes. I accept the fact that the important painting of the last hundred years was done in France. American painters have generally missed the point of modern painting from beginning to end. (The only American master who interests me is Ryder.) Thus the fact that good European moderns are now here is very important, for they bring with them an understanding of the problems of modern painting. I am particularly impressed with their concept of the source of art being the unconscious. This idea interests me more than these specific painters do, for the two artists I admire most, Picasso and Miró, are still abroad.

Do you think there can be a purely American art?
The idea of an isolated American painting, so popular in this country during the 'thirties, seems absurd to me, just as the idea of creating a purely American mathematics or physics would seem absurd . . . And in another sense, the problem doesn't exist at all; or, if it did, would solve itself: An American is an American and his painting would naturally be qualified by that fact, whether he wills it or not. But the basic problems of contemporary painting are independent of any one country.

On April 14 Pollock wrote to Charles:

I have just got my contract set for next year—so am a little more at ease. I have really had amazing success for the first year of showing—a color reproduction in the April *Harpers Bazaar*—and reproductions in the *Arts and Architecture*.

May 2. After some months of deliberation the Acquisitions Committee of The Museum of Modern Art decided to act on the recommendation of Alfred Barr and bought *The She-Wolf* for the Museum's collection. This was the first Pollock to be purchased by a museum.

p. 86

In May Pollock reported to Charles:

I am getting $150 a month from the gallery, which just about doesn't meet the bills. I will have to sell a lot of work thru the year to get it above $150. The Museum of Modern Art bought the painting reproduced in *Harpers* this week, which I hope will stimulate further sales.

Sometime the same month Putzel wrote Pollock:

Mrs. Lloyd, of Haverford, Pa., came in to see the (sold) long drawing and was really enthusiastic. She'll get one, ultimately. Dr. Morley of the S.F. Museum went to see "Male and Female" at Pinacotheca, and will bring back some S.F. Museum trustees. Probably—possibly, I mean—you may be really launched by the beginning of '45, and much more solidly or enduringly than sales pressure and advertising could have effected, and with no need for social playing up.

p. 87

During the summer Pollock and Lee Krasner rented a studio on Back Street in Provincetown. They were joined for two weeks by Putzel, who had just left Art of This Century and was planning to open his 67 Gallery in October.

From about the fall and continuing into the next year Pollock experimented with graphic art and worked intermittently at Stanley William Hayter's Atelier 17.

p. 86

In November Sidney Janis' book, *Abstract & Surrealist Art in America,* was published, which included a statement by Pollock about *The She-Wolf*:

> *She-Wolf* came into existence because I had to paint it. Any attempt on my part to say something about it, to attempt explanation of the inexplicable, could only destroy it.

p. 88

February 8–March 12. Cincinnati Art Museum. ABSTRACT AND SURREALIST ART IN THE UNITED STATES. 1 painting: *The Guardians of the Secret.* Sidney Janis selected the material for this circulating exhibition, the San Francisco Museum of Art published the catalogue (January 1944) and organized the details of the tour, which continued through July and included Denver, Seattle, Santa Barbara, and San Francisco. Pollock was shown in the group called "American Surrealist Painters."

February 1944–May 1945. TWELVE CONTEMPORARY PAINTERS. 2 paintings: *The Moon-Woman Cuts the Circle, The She-Wolf.* An exhibition organized by the Department of Circulating Exhibitions of The Museum of Modern Art, New York, which made a tour of universities and museums throughout the country. Among other painters shown were Darrel Austin, Matta, Arshile Gorky, Morris Graves, and Andrew Wyeth.

James Johnson Sweeney, "Five American Painters" (*Harper's Bazaar,* April). Pollock included, with Matta, Gorky, Graves, and Milton Avery. *The She-Wolf* was reproduced in color.

p. 86

April 11–May 6. Art of This Century, New York. FIRST EXHIBITION IN AMERICA OF [20 paintings]. 1 painting: *Pasiphaë.* An exhibition of a group of abstract paintings never before shown in America. Among the painters shown were Braque, Dali, Ernst, Kandinsky, Léger, Masson, Matta, Miró, Motherwell, Picasso, Rothko, and Tanguy.

p. 87

May 9–27. The Pinacotheca, New York. GROUP EXHIBITION. 1 painting: *Male and Female.* Among other painters shown: Byron Browne, Willem de Kooning, George L. K. Morris.

November 29–December 30. Mortimer Brandt Gallery, New York. ABSTRACT AND SURREALIST ART IN AMERICA. 1 painting: *The Mad Moon-Woman.* A selection of painters and paintings, with some changes, from the traveling exhibition organized by Sidney Janis.

1945

Pollock and Lee Krasner first visited East Hampton during the week of August 6, when they accompanied Reuben Kadish and his wife who were looking for a house to purchase.

Miss Krasner suggested to Pollock that they rent a house there for the winter, but he considered this out of the question. About a week later, however, upon their return to the city, he changed his mind and decided to give up the apartment and move to Long Island. Sometime in the early fall they returned to East Hampton to look for a suitable home. They found a comfortable farmhouse with about five acres of land and a large barn on Fireplace Road in Springs, for $5,000. After some persuasion by Miss Krasner and on the advice of the collector W. N. M. Davis, Peggy Guggenheim lent them $2,000 for the down payment and worked out a new, two-year contract with Pollock. She raised his stipend to $300 a month, less a deduction toward repayment of the loan. In exchange, Pollock was to give her his total output.

On October 25 Pollock married Lee Krasner. He insisted on a church wedding, which took place at the Marble Collegiate Church on Fifth Avenue and was witnessed by May Natalie Tabak [Mrs. Harold Rosenberg].

In November the Pollocks moved into their new home at Springs. By Thanksgiving they were sufficiently settled to invite Pollock's family for dinner.

February. The David Porter Gallery, Washington, D.C. A PAINTING PROPHECY—1950. Number and titles of works not known. "Most of the artists represented in this exhibition

LEFT: Jackson and Lee Pollock, East Hampton, 1949

RIGHT: Jackson and Lee Pollock in front of their house in Springs, 1949

do not work in representational realism; they are seeking to express their personal verities in a manner which is beyond realism. . . . It is the feeling of this Gallery that these painters will become increasingly important as time allows for a greater appreciation of this art." Among those included in this exhibition, which was offered for circulation to other galleries and museums, were William Baziotes, Gorky, Adolph Gottlieb, de Kooning, Motherwell, Rothko, and Bradley Walker Tomlin.

pp. 28, 31, 86-88

March 5–31. The Arts Club of Chicago. One-man show. 17 paintings, 8 drawings. Paintings: *The Moon-Woman, The Guardians of the Secret, Search for a Symbol, Stenographic Figure, Wounded Animal, Pasiphaë, The Mad Moon-Woman, Male and Female, The Magic Mirror,* and 8 Untitled; drawings: 8 Untitled. The catalogue essay was a reprint of James Johnson Sweeney's text in the 1943 Art of This Century catalogue.

ELEANOR JEWETT (*Chicago Daily Tribune,* March 6)
Jackson Pollock . . . fills the first galleries with his effusive abstractions, which apparently owe a little to the influence of Edward Lear. . . . His chief trouble seems to be that his trumpet has gone wild and he is sounding in all directions at once, like a weather vane in a high wind whirling in mad circles. His paintings seem based on the theory that the more childishly scribbled they are the more significant they are. He suggests in "Pasiphaë" the "Guernica" of Picasso, but his ruins are more complete. . . . His colors are violent and the atmosphere of the exhibit is definitely restless and raucous.

p. 90

March 10–April 8. Cincinnati Art Museum. THE CRITICS' CHOICE OF CONTEMPORARY AMERICAN PAINTING, 49TH ANNUAL. 1 painting: *Gothic.* "Chosen by Clement Greenberg, *The Nation.* Lent by Art of This Century."

pp. 89-93

March 19–April 14. Art of This Century, New York. One-man show. Gouaches, drawings, and 13 paintings: *Horizontal on Black, Square on Black, The Totem–Lesson I, The Totem–Lesson II, The Night Dancer, The First Dream, Portrait of H.M., Night Ceremony, Night Mist, Two, There Were Seven in Eight, Night Magic, Image.* Opening-day visitors were "invited to view a Mural . . . from 3 to 6, at 155 East 61st Street. 1st Floor."

HOWARD DEVREE (*New York Times,* March 25)
These big, sprawling coloramas impress me as being surcharged with violent emotional reaction which never is clarified enough in the expression to establish true communication with the observer. Only "The Night Dancer" of the current crop conveys to me any intended message. "There Were Seven in Eight" as a title is purely cryptic understatement; and one or two of the other paintings might as well be called "explosion in a shingle mill," with their pother of paint and flying forms.

CLEMENT GREENBERG (*Nation,* April 7)
Jackson Pollock's second one-man show at Art of This Century . . . establishes him, in my opinion, as the strongest painter of his generation and perhaps the greatest one to appear since Miró. The

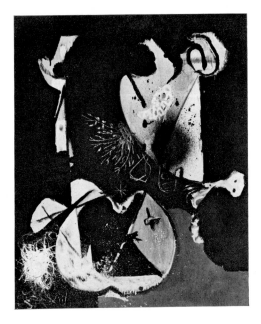

Painting. (1945?) Gouache on plywood, 23 x 18⅞ inches. The Museum of Modern Art, New York, gift of Monroe Wheeler

only optimism in his smoky, turbulent painting comes from his own manifest faith in the efficacy, for him personally, of art. There has been a certain amount of self-deception in School of Paris art since the exit of cubism. In Pollock there is absolutely none, and he is not afraid to look ugly—all profoundly original art looks ugly at first. Those who find his oils overpowering are advised to approach him through his gouaches, which in trying less to wring every possible ounce of intensity from every square inch of surface achieve greater clarity and are less suffocatingly packed than the oils. Among the latter, however, are two—both called Totem Lessons—for which I cannot find strong enough words of praise. Pollock's single fault is not that he crowds his canvases too evenly but that he sometimes juxtaposes colors and values so abruptly that gaping holes are created.

PARKER TYLER (*View,* May)
The nervous, if rough, calligraphy of Pollock's work may hide a protest against the cool architectural objectivity of the abstractionist mode as it makes its subjective statement. Pollock does not seem to be especially talented, there being too much of an air of baked-macaroni about some of his patterns, as though they were scrambled baroque designs. But he has a strong feeling for matière and on occasion is an interesting colorist.

MANNY FARBER (*New Republic,* June 25)
The painting of Jackson Pollock, which has been called untalented and likened to "baked macaroni" in *View* and to an "exploison in a shingle-mill" in the New York *Times,* has been, in at least three paintings I have seen, both masterful and miraculous. The three paintings include a wild abstraction twenty-six feet long, commissioned by Miss Peggy Guggenheim for the hallway of her home, and two gouache drawings being exhibited at Art of This Century. The mural is . . . an almost incredible success. It is violent in its expression, endlessly fascinating in detail, without superficiality, and so well ordered that it composes the wall in a quiet, contained, buoyant way. Pollock's aim in painting seems to be to express feeling that ranges from pleasant enthusiasm through wildness to explosiveness, as purely and as well as possible. The mode is . . . one that stems from Miró and Picasso but is a step farther in abstraction. The style is very personal and, unlike that of many painters of this period, the individuality is in the way the medium is used rather than in the peculiarities of subject matter. . . .

Implicit in the change from naturalism to abstraction in painting is the change in attitude about surface: The surface is no longer considered as something to be designed into an approximation of a naturalistic, three-dimensional world, but, more realistically, is considered simply as flat, opaque and bounded. Pollock's work explores the possibilities and the character of horizontal design. . . . His manner of building form and surface out rather than in has produced original, dramatic and decorative effects, and the painting as a whole demonstrates again that abstract art can be as voluptuous as Renaissance painting.

May 14–July 7. 67 Gallery, New York. A PROBLEM FOR CRITICS. Number and titles of works not known. An exhibition organized by Howard Putzel in which he tried to define a recent tendency in painting, which he called "a new metamorphism," whose real forerunners, he believed, were Arp and Miró. In referring to the American artists he had selected, he remarked, "I believe we see real American painting beginning now." Among those in the exhibition were Arp, Gorky, Gottlieb, Hans Hofmann, Lee Krasner, Masson, Miró, Picasso, R. W. Pousette-Dart, Mark Rothko, Charles Seliger, and Rufino Tamayo.

May 17–June 17. California Palace of the Legion of Honor, San Francisco. CONTEMPORARY AMERICAN PAINTING EXHIBITION. 1 painting: *The Magic Mirror*. Exhibition organized by Jermayne MacAgy with the assistance of Daniel Catton Rich.

August 7–26. San Francisco Museum of Art. One-man show. Almost exactly the same exhibition as that held at the Arts Club of Chicago in March.

> ALFRED FRANKENSTEIN (*San Francisco Chronicle*, August 12)
> A few of Jackson Pollock's canvases have been out this way before and they have always made a very striking and positive impression. This solo assemblage is even more impressive because it provides a fairly well rounded idea of what he is all about.
>
> He is one of the most vibrant and exciting, nervous, flaming and brilliant painters now at work in this country. His pictures are almost entirely nonrepresentational, but his abstraction has nothing to do with geometry; the flare and spatter and fury of his paintings are emotional rather than formal, and like the best jazz, one feels that much of it is the result of inspired improvisation rather than conscious planning. Nevertheless, for all its fury of movement, its heated color and its tangled complexity of line, this painting holds together. There is a grand swirling heave that organizes the canvas; sometimes there is a counterpoint of swirls like a baroque design. It carries, too; Pollock is as strong from a distance as he is close to.

1946

Pollock turned an upstairs bedroom of the new house into a temporary studio and prepared for his third show at Art of This Century. About this time he designed the dust jacket for Peggy Guggenheim's first book of memoirs, *Out of This Century*.

During the summer the large barn was moved from directly behind the farmhouse to the north side of the property and fixed up as Pollock's studio. Lee took over the bedroom as hers.

p. 92

April 2–20. Art of This Century, New York. One-man show. 19 paintings. 11 oils: *Circumcision, Water Figure, The Troubled Queen, The Little King, The Child Proceeds, The White Angel, An Ace in the Hole, Direction, Moon Vessel, High Priestess, Once Upon a Time;* and 8 temperas.

> CLEMENT GREENBERG (*Nation*, April 13)
> What is thought to be Pollock's bad taste is in reality simply his willingness to be ugly in terms of contemporary taste. In the course of time this ugliness will become a new standard of beauty. Besides, Pollock submits to a habit of discipline derived from cubism; and even as he goes away

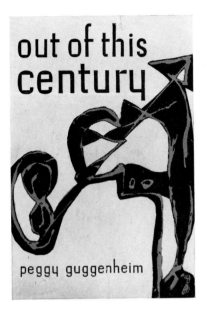

Jacket designed by Pollock for Peggy Guggenheim's book of memoirs, *Out of This Century*, 1946 (front and back)

from cubism he carries with him the unity of style with which it endowed him when in the beginning he put himself under its influence. Thus Pollock's superiority to his contemporaries in this country lies in his ability to create a genuinely violent and extravagant art without losing stylistic control. His emotion starts out pictorially; it does not have to be castrated and translated in order to be put into a picture. . . .

One has to learn Pollock's idiom to realize its flexibility. And it is precisely because I am, in general, still learning from Pollock that I hesitate to attempt a more thorough analysis of his art.

BEN WOLF (*Art Digest,* April 15)
Pollock suffers from [the] ability to achieve surface virtuosity that in the final analysis frequently forbids him to the promised land of plastic realization. The artist has the requisite equipment to cross that "last river," but somehow seems to prefer to dangle his toes in the warmer water along the shore of his facility.

December 10, 1946–January 16, 1947. Whitney Museum of American Art, New York. ANNUAL EXHIBITION OF CONTEMPORARY AMERICAN PAINTING. 1 painting: *Two.* Pollock's first participation in the Whitney annuals.

CLEMENT GREENBERG (*Nation,* December 28)
The best painting at the present show is Jackson Pollock's "Two." Those who think I exaggerate Pollock's merit are invited to compare this large vertical canvas with everything else in the Annual.

1947

Pollock spent most of the year at Springs painting.

At the end of the season Peggy Guggenheim closed her gallery and planned to return to Europe. She had trouble finding a dealer to take over Pollock's contract, but finally in May Betty Parsons signed an agreement with Miss Guggenheim to handle Pollock's works until Miss Guggenheim's contract with him would run out early in 1948. During this period Miss Guggenheim was to receive the proceeds from the sale of paintings she still owned and would continue to pay Pollock a monthly allowance. Until the contract expired all of Pollock's new paintings were to become her property, though she allowed him to retain one painting a year. The agreement also stipulated that Mrs. Parsons would give Pollock a one-man show the following winter.

In applying for a Guggenheim Fellowship during this year, Pollock made the following statement:

I intend to paint large movable pictures which will function between the easel and mural. I have set a precedent in this genre in a large painting for Miss Peggy Guggenheim which was installed in her house and was later shown in the "Large Scale Paintings" show at the Museum of Modern Art. It is at present on loan at Yale University.

I believe the easel picture to be a dying form, and the tendency of modern feeling is towards the wall picture or mural. I believe the time is not yet ripe for a *full* transition from easel to mural. The pictures I contemplate painting would constitute a halfway state, and an attempt to point out the direction of the future, without arriving there completely.

He wrote the following remarks for the first, and only, issue of *Possibilities* (1947/48) edited by Robert Motherwell and Harold Rosenberg:

My painting does not come from the easel. I hardly ever stretch my canvas before painting. I prefer to tack the unstretched canvas to the hard wall or the floor. I need the resistance of a hard surface. On the floor I am more at ease. I feel nearer, more a part of the painting, since this way I can walk around it, work from the four sides and literally be *in* the painting. This is akin to the method of the Indian sand painters of the West.

I continue to get further away from the usual painter's tools such as easel, palette, brushes, etc. I prefer sticks, trowels, knives and dripping fluid paint or a heavy impasto with sand, broken glass and other foreign matter added.

When I am *in* my painting, I'm not aware of what I'm doing. It is only after a sort of "get acquainted" period that I see what I have been about. I have no fears about making changes, destroying the image, etc., because the painting has a life of its own. I try to let it come through. It is only when I lose contact with the painting that the result is a mess. Otherwise there is pure harmony, an easy give and take, and the painting comes out well.

In his draft for this statement, he also said:

The source of my painting is the unconscious. I approach painting the same way I approach drawing. That is direct—with no preliminary studies. The drawings I do are relative to my painting but not for it.

In December Pollock signed a contract with Betty Parsons effective through June 1949.

January 14–February 1. Art of This Century, New York. One-man show. 16 paintings: Two series: *Sounds in the Grass* and *Accabonac Creek*. *Sounds in the Grass* included *Croaking Movement*, *Shimmering Substance*, *Eyes in the Heat*, *Earth Worms*, *The Blue Unconscious*, *Something of the Past*, and *The Dancers*. *Accabonac Creek* included *The Water Bull*, *Yellow Triangle*, *Bird Effort*, *Gray Center*, *The Key*, *Constellation*, *The Tea Cup*, *Magic Light*. Also included was Miss Guggenheim's *Mural*. The catalogue note was by [W.] N. M. Davis:

pp. 90-91

You can see "The She-Wolf" many times at the Museum of Modern Art and you are never disappointed; in Jackson Pollock's work there is the quality that challenges. With Pollock, one is constantly learning. In the past four years he has been showing pictures that cannot be considered as less than the best in current American painting.

The present show finds Pollock working in perhaps a somewhat gayer mood. In this exhibit he maintains the high level and the integrity that stamp all his painting: like "The She-Wolf", these pictures should be seen many many times.

p. 86

CLEMENT GREENBERG (*Nation*, February 1)
Jackson Pollock's fourth one-man show in so many years . . . is his best since his first one and signals what may be a major step in his development—which I regard as the most important so far of the younger generation of American painters. He has now largely abandoned his customary heavy black-and-whitish or gun-metal chiaroscuro for the higher scales, for alizarins, cream-whites, cerulean blues, pinks, and sharp greens. Like Dubuffet, however, whose art goes in a similar if less abstract direction, Pollock remains essentially a draftsman in black and white who must as a rule rely on these colors to maintain the consistency and power of surface of his pictures. As is the case with almost all post-cubist painting of any real originality, it is the tension inherent in the constructed, re-created flatness of the surface that produces the strength of his art. . . .

Pollock has gone beyond the stage where he needs to make his poetry explicit in ideographs. What he invents instead has perhaps, in its very abstractness and absence of assignable definition, a more reverberating meaning. He is American and rougher and more brutal, but he is also completer. In any case he is certainly less conservative, less of an easel-painter in the traditional sense than Dubuffet. . . . Pollock points a way beyond the easel, beyond the mobile, framed picture, to the mural, perhaps—or perhaps not. I cannot tell.

April 1–May 4. The Museum of Modern Art, New York. LARGE SCALE MODERN PAINTINGS. 1 painting: *Mural*.

pp. 90-91

Summer. *Mural* loaned to Yale University Art Gallery.

September 25–27. Winchester, England. C.S.A. LOAN EXHIBITION OF MODERN ART. 1 work: *Abstraction* (Collection Arthur Jeffress).

CLEMENT GREENBERG, "The Present Prospects of American Painting and Sculpture" (*Horizon* [London], October)
Significantly and peculiarly, the most powerful painter in contemporary America and the only one who promises to be a major one is a Gothic, morbid and extreme disciple of Picasso's Cubism and Miró's post-Cubism, tinctured also with Kandinsky and Surrealist inspiration. His name is Jackson Pollock, and if the aspect of his art is not as originally and uniquely local as that of Graves' and Tobey's, the feeling it contains is perhaps even more radically American. . . . Pollock's strength lies in the emphatic surfaces of his pictures, which it is his concern to maintain and intensify in all that thick, fuliginous flatness which began—but only began—to be the strong point of late Cubism. Of no profound originality as a colourist, Pollock draws massively, laying on paint directly from

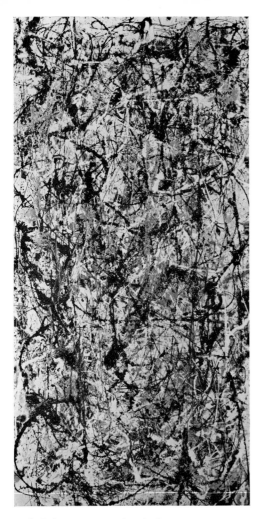

Cathedral. 1947. Enamel and aluminum paint on canvas, 71 x 35 inches. Dallas Museum of Fine Arts, gift of Mr. and Mrs. Bernard J. Reis

pp. 90, 96, 99

the tube, and handles black, white and grey as they have not been handled since Gris' middle period. No other abstract painter since Cubism has been so well able to retain classical chiaroscuro.

For all its Gothic quality, Pollock's art is still an attempt to cope with urban life; it dwells entirely in the lonely jungle of immediate sensations, impulses and notions, therefore is positivist, concrete. Yet its Gothic-ness, its paranoia and resentment narrow it; large though it may be in ambition—large enough to contain inconsistencies, ugliness, blind spots and monotonous passages—it nevertheless lacks breadth.

November 6, 1947–January 11, 1948. The Art Institute of Chicago. ABSTRACT AND SURREALIST AMERICAN ART. THE FIFTY-EIGHTH ANNUAL EXHIBITION OF AMERICAN PAINTING AND SCULPTURE. 1 painting: *The Key*.

"The Best?" (*Time*, December 1). A short item attempted to ridicule Greenberg's statements by reproducing a work by Pollock, the point being that the abstract quality of this canvas was sufficient to prove that its creator was not worth noting.

December 6, 1947–January 25, 1948. Whitney Museum of American Art, New York. ANNUAL EXHIBITION OF CONTEMPORARY AMERICAN PAINTING. 1 painting: *Galaxy*.

1948

In April Betty Parsons wrote to Peggy Guggenheim of the "terrible financial condition of the Pollocks."

In May Pollock took part in a protest meeting at The Museum of Modern Art directed against certain art critics and, especially, a manifesto issued by the Boston Institute of Contemporary Art that accused advanced art of "obscurity and negation" and questioned the honesty of its practitioners.

In June Pollock was notified that he had been selected as the beneficiary to receive the income—$1,500 to be paid in quarterly installments between July 1948 and July 1949—of the Eben Demarest Trust Fund, which had been created for the general purpose of the advancement of art and archaeology. This grant was secured with the assistance of James Johnson Sweeney.

In the fall Pollock entered treatment with a general practitioner at East Hampton who was able to arrest his alcoholism. Pollock was to remain "on the wagon" until the fall of 1950.

January 5–23. Betty Parsons Gallery, New York. One-man show. 17 paintings: *Enchanted Forest, Cathedral, Lucifer, Vortex, Phosphorescence, Unfounded, Gothic, Shooting Star, Sea Change, Full Fathom Five, Comet, Magic Lantern, Watery Paths, Prism, The Nest, Alchemy,*

Reflections of the Big Dipper. Lee and Jackson Pollock hung this show as well as others at Parsons, often with the help of friends such as Herbert Matter, Barnett Newman, Tony Smith, and Clyfford Still.

A[LONZO] L[ANSFORD] (*Art Digest*, January 15)
At least two foremost critics here and in England have recently included Pollock in their lists of the half-dozen most important of America's "advanced" painters; other equally prestigeous authorities have dismissed him, at least verbally, with an oath. . . .

Pollock has said that Thomas Benton was a good teacher because he taught him how not to paint like Benton; that he doesn't is startlingly patent. Pollock's current method seems to be a sort of automatism; apparently, while staring steadily up into the sky, he lets go a loaded brush on the canvas, rapidly swirling and looping and wriggling till the paint runs out. Then he repeats the procedure with another color, and another, till the canvas is covered. This, with much use of aluminum paint, results in a colorful and exciting panel. Probably it also results in the severest pain in the neck since Michaelangelo painted the Sistine Ceiling.

ROBERT M. COATES (*New Yorker*, January 17)
Pollock is much harder to understand than most of his confreres. The main thing one gets from his work is an impression of tremendous energy, expressed in huge blobs of color alternating with lacings and interlacings of fine lines. Recognizable symbols are almost nonexistent, and he attempts to create by sheer color and movement the mood or atmosphere he wants to convey. Such a style has its dangers, for the threads of communication between artist and spectator are so very tenuous that the utmost attention is required to get the message through. There are times when communications break down entirely, and, with the best will in the world, I can say of such pieces as "Lucifer," "Reflection of the Big Dipper," and "Cathedral" only that they seem mere unorganized explosions of random energy, and therefore meaningless. I liked, though, his "Full Fathom Five," with its crusted greens and whites overlaid by black swirls, and "Sea Change," while both "Magic Lantern" and the larger "Enchanted Forest" have a good deal of poetic suggestion about them.

CLEMENT GREENBERG (*Nation*, January 24)
As before, his new work offers a puzzle to all those not sincerely in touch with contemporary painting. I already hear: "wallpaper patterns," "the picture does not finish inside the canvas," "raw, uncultivated emotion," and so on, and so on. Since Mondrian no one has driven the easel picture quite so far away from itself; but this is not altogether Pollock's own doing. In this day and age the art of painting increasingly rejects the easel and yearns for the wall. It is Pollock's culture as a painter that has made him so sensitive and receptive to a tendency that has brought with it, in his case, a greater concentration on surface texture and tactile qualities, to balance the danger of monotony that arises from the even, all-over design which has become Pollock's consistent practice. . . .

It is indeed a mark of Pollock's powerful originality that he should present problems in judgment that must await the digestion of each new phase of his development before they can be solved. Since Marin—with whom Pollock will in time be able to compete for recognition as the greatest American painter of the twentieth century—no other American artist has presented such a case.

January 31–March 21. Whitney Museum of American Art, New York. ANNUAL EXHIBITION OF CONTEMPORARY AMERICAN SCULPTURE, WATERCOLORS, AND DRAWINGS. 1 watercolor: *Dancing Forms*.

May 29–September 30. Venice. XXIV BIENNALE: LA COLLEZIONE PEGGY GUGGENHEIM. 6 works, listed in the official catalogue as: *Eyes in the Heat, The Moon-Woman, Two, Circumcision, Drawing, Don Quixote*. Miss Guggenheim's own catalogue, with forewords by Bruno Alfieri, Herbert Read, Jean Arp, and Max Ernst, omits the *Don Quixote* and lists instead a gouache of 1946.

p. 42

"A Life Round Table on Modern Art" (*Life*, October 11)
Pollock's *Cathedral* was championed by Mr. [Clement] Greenberg who thought it a first-class example of Pollock's work, and one of the best paintings recently produced in this country. Mr. Georges Duthuit [then Editor of *Transition Forty-Eight*] said, "I find it quite lovely. It is new to me . . . a contemporary composer playing on his sensations." Sir Leigh Ashton [then Director of the Victoria and Albert Museum, London] said, "It seems to me exquisite in tone and quality. It would make a most enchanting printed silk. But I cannot see why it is called the *Cathedral*. It is exquisitely painted and the color is ravishing, but I do not think it has structural design."

Mr. [Francis Henry] Taylor [then Director of The Metropolitan Museum of Art] found it "very lovely." Mr. [Aldous] Huxley was less impressed. Said he, "It raises a question of why it stops when it does. The artist could go on forever. (Laughter) I don't know. It seems to me like a panel for a wallpaper which is repeated indefinitely around the wall." Mr. [Alfred] Frankfurter [then Editor of *Art News*] said he was no admirer of Pollock but thought this work remarkably good if compared with a lot of abstract painting that is being turned out nowadays. Mr. [James Johnson] Sweeney thought it had "spontaneity," "freedom," "expression," "a sense of textured surface," and "linear organization." Mr. [A. Hyatt] Mayor [then Curator of Prints, The Metropolitan Museum of Art] remarked, "I suspect any picture I think I could have made myself." Dr. [Theodore] Greene [Professor of Philosophy, Yale University] said it left him completely cold and seemed "a pleasant design for a necktie."

November 30, 1948–January 16, 1949. California Palace of the Legion of Honor, San Francisco. THIRD ANNUAL EXHIBITION OF CONTEMPORARY PAINTING. 1 painting: *Cathedral*.

1949

On January 10 Pollock's mother wrote from Deep River, Connecticut, where she was staying with Sanford, to Charles in East Lansing, Michigan:

Jack and Lee were here and we had a very nice Christmas. . . . And there was no drinking. We were all so happy. Jack has been going to a Dr. in Hampton and hadn't drank anything for over three weeks at Christmas hope he will stay with it he says he wants to quit and went to the Dr. on his own. the Dr. told him he would have to leave it alone

Pollock at the potter's wheel in Mrs. Larkin's studio, East Hampton, winter 1949/50

everything wine to beer for they were poison to him. He has a Ford Coupe now and he shouldn't drive unless he stops liquor. The Dr. says it is up to him. When he has his show will be a test and a hard one for Jack. If he can go through that without drinking will be something I hope he can and will. Will be glad when the show is over and he is home again.

In the same month Peggy Guggenheim described to Betty Parsons her unsuccessful attempts to get Pollock a one-man show in Paris.

About the time of his second show at the Parsons Gallery (January–February), Pollock met the painter Alfonso Ossorio.

In mid-April Stella Pollock wrote Charles of a visit she had made to East Hampton:

> Was . . . out at Jack and Lee was so nice to be there and see them so happy and no drinking he can serve liquor to others He feels so much better says so they were getting ready to put in garden they have good soil Lee loves to dig in the dirt and she has green fingers Jack is going to shingle his studio prices have dropped enough that he feels he can he will do it himself

Toward the end of June Pollock renewed his contract with Betty Parsons, to run through January 1, 1952.

During the summer Pollock made several abstract terra-cotta sculptures with the assistance of Mrs. Lawrence Larkin, a neighbor at East Hampton who was a potter.

About this time Pollock decided to forego titling his works and to number them instead (although later, certain paintings that had originally been numbered were given titles, e.g., *Number 10, 1952* became *Convergence; Number 11, 1952* became *Blue Poles*). The numbers seldom indicate the precise sequence in which the works were painted, and there is some duplication of numbers in some years.

January 24–February 12. Betty Parsons Gallery, New York. One-man show. 26 works numbered 1 to 26, all 1948, some with descriptive titles. On canvas: *Number 1* (*Aluminum, Black, White*), *Number 2* [*Shadows*], *Number 3*, *Number 5*, *Number 7* (*Black and Red*), *Number 8*, *Number 9* [*Summertime*], *Number 10* [*The Wooden Horse*], *Number 11*, *Number 13* [*Arabesque*], *Number 16*, *Number 18* (*Black, Red, Yellow*), *Number 24* [*White Cockatoo*], *Number 25*, *Number 26*; on paper: *Number 4* (*Gray and Red*), *Number 6* (*Blue, Red, Yellow*), *Number 12* (*Yellow, Gray, Black*), *Number 14* (*Gray*), *Number 15* (*Red, Gray, White, Yellow*), *Number 17*, *Number 19*, *Number 20*, *Number 21*, *Number 22*, *Number 23*.

pp. 47, 65, 97-98, 101

SAM HUNTER (*New York Times*, January 30)
Jackson Pollock's show . . . certainly reflects an advanced stage of the disintegration of the modern painting. But it is disintegration with a possibly liberating and cathartic effect and informed by a highly individual rhythm. It would seem that the main intention of these curiously webbed linear variations . . . is a deliberate assault on our image-making faculty. At every point of concentration of these high-tension moments of bravura phrasing (which visually are like agitated coils of barbed wire) there is a disappointing absence of resolution in an image or pictorial incident. . . .

Even in his case the work is not perhaps sufficiently sustained by a unifying or major theme . . . and is too prodigal with clusters of surrealist intuitions. What does emerge is the large scale of Pollock's operations, his highly personal rhythm and finally something like a pure calligraphic metaphor for a ravaging, aggressive virility.

(*Time*, February 7)
A Jackson Pollock painting is apt to resemble a child's contour map of the Battle of Gettysburg . . . Nevertheless, he is the darling of a highbrow cult which considers him "the most powerful painter in America."

EMILY GENAUER (*New York World-Telegram*, February 7)
Most of Jackson Pollock's paintings, at the Betty Parsons Gallery, resemble nothing so much as a mop of tangled hair I have an irresistible urge to comb out. One or two of them manage to be organized and interesting. Those called, "Blue, red, yellow," and "Yellow, gray, black," because of their less "accidental" development and their spatial depth, suggest how good a painter Pollock could really be.

PAUL MOCSANYI (*United Press Red Letter*, February 9)
Pollock simply enumerates the colors and materials used. Thus he emphasizes that the interplay of color and material has replaced the subject in his paintings. His 68 x 104 inch "No. 1," described as "Aluminum, black, white, oil on canvas, horizontal," is covered by whirling black and white lines. Against this maddening movement large quiet spaces are built up in shades from white to black. This combination of the ecstatic and the monumental is not without a certain grandeur.

CLEMENT GREENBERG (*Nation*, February 19)
Jackson Pollock's show this year . . . continued his astounding progress. His confidence in his gift appears to be almost enough of itself to cancel out or suppress his limitations—which, especially in regard to color, are certainly there. One large picture, "Number One," which carries the idea of last year's brilliant "Cathedral" more than a few steps farther, quieted any doubts this reviewer may have felt—and he does not in all honesty remember having felt many—as to the justness of the superlatives with which he has praised Pollock's art in the past. I do not know of any other painting by an American that I could safely put next to this huge baroque scrawl in aluminum, black, white, madder, and blue . . . the general quality that emerged . . . seemed more than enough to justify the claim that Pollock is one of the major painters of our time.

E[LAINE DE] K[OONING] (*Art News*, March)
Jackson Pollock's new abstractions, violent in drawing and in application of pigment, are paradoxically tranquil in expression. Here, complex, luminous networks . . . give an impression of

Number 1, 1948. Oil on canvas, 5 feet 8 inches x 8 feet 8 inches. The Museum of Modern Art, New York

being frozen in position. His flying lines are spattered on in intense, unmixed colors to create wiry, sculptural constructions, which stand immobile and apart, uninvolved with the backgrounds.

Letter of April 4 from the French painter Georges Mathieu to Betty Parsons:

In a recent issue of ART NEWS, I saw that there has just been an exhibition of the works of Jackson POLLOCK in your gallery.

I consider Pollock as the greatest living American painter, and I would like to devote to him an article in a review I am about to launch. Also, a friend of mine would like to include a few pages about him in a book he is going to write about some tendencies of contemporary painting.

February 19–March 10. La Strozzina, Strozzi Palace, Florence. LA COLLEZIONE GUGGENHEIM. 10 works: Drawing (1942), *The Moon-Woman, Two, Don Quixote, Circumcision, Bird Effort, Sounds in the Grass [Croaking Movement], Eyes in the Heat,* 2 gouaches (both 1946). Because of limited space Miss Guggenheim's collection was shown in three consecutive exhibitions: Cubist and Abstract Painters, Dadaist and Surrealist Painters, and Younger Painters. Pollock was shown with the third group. In June the exhibition traveled to Milan where it was shown in the Palazzo Reale under the auspices of L'Associazone Artisti Italiani; catalogue foreword by Francesco Flora.

Untitled. (1949). Painted terra cotta, 8 inches long. Estate of the artist

pp. 102-5

February 27–April 3. University of Illinois. EXHIBITION OF CONTEMPORARY AMERICAN PAINTING. 1 painting: *Galaxy*.

July 7–26. Guild Hall, East Hampton. SEVENTEEN ARTISTS. 1 painting: title not known. An exhibition of works by painters and sculptors living in and around the tip of Long Island, it included, among others, David Burliuk, George Constant, Balcomb Greene, Lee Krasner, Julian Levi, Moses Soyer, Raphael Soyer.

August 3–October 5. The Museum of Modern Art, New York. SCULPTURE BY PAINTERS. 2 works: *Drawing Number 4, 1948* (oil on paper), and an untitled terra cotta. The exhibition, organized for the Department of Circulating Exhibitions by Jane Sabersky, was first shown at the Museum, and then circulated to 12 cities in the United States, November 1949– May 1951.

September 14–October 3. Samuel M. Kootz Gallery, New York. THE INTRASUBJECTIVES. 1 painting: Untitled. The exhibition, whose title came from a phrase taken from Ortega y Gasset, also included Baziotes, Gorky, Gottlieb, Graves, Hofmann, de Kooning, Motherwell, Reinhardt, Rothko, Tobey, and Tomlin. Catalogue texts were by Samuel Kootz and Harold Rosenberg.

November 21–December 10. Betty Parsons Gallery, New York. One-man show. 34 oils on paper and canvas, all 1949, titled respectively, *Number 1, 2, 3, 4, 5, 7* [*Out of the Web*], *8, 9, 10, 11, 12, 13, 14, 15, 16, 17, 18, 19, 20, 21, 22, 23, 24, 25, 26, 27, 28, 29, 30* [*Birds of Paradise*], *31, 32, 33, 34, 35* [*Mural*(?)]. A special feature of this exhibition was a model of a museum for Pollock's paintings designed by his friend Peter Blake. The exhibition announcement read: "Murals in Modern Architecture. A Theatrical Exercise Using Jackson Pollock's Paintings and Sculpture. By Peter Blake." Pollock made several small wire-and-plaster sculptures for the model.

CARLYLE BURROWS (*Herald Tribune*, November 27)
. . . a group of elaborately interwoven color compositions. . . . Wholly non-objective, it is the simple interplay of their color, combined with line of rhythmic intensity that fascinates. Mr. Pollock, it seems apparent, is finding it difficult to extend his range in the method of painting he has so confidently developed. While the designs are varied enough in color their form appears—in a large display—more than ever repetitious.

STUART PRESTON (*New York Times,* November 27)
There is a world of difference between the dazzling purity of [Kandinsky] and the torrential downpour of pigment that heaves and sways on [Pollock's] canvases, turning expressionist means to work for abstractionist ends. Color is Pollock's forte. In the dense web of paint that weaves back and forth it is remarkable how the silvers, blacks, whites and yellows stand on their own instead

of killing each other. In the very biggest canvases the myriad tiny climaxes of paint and color fail to add up to an over-all design, but in the long narrow ones a pleasingly large repeat design gathers momentum as it moves from left to right. And in No. 23 a spider web of black draws a pattern, elegant as a Chinese character. In such work is ground for further development, rather than in those heavy with the medium alone.

A[MY] R[OBINSON] (*Art News*, December)
Jackson Pollock . . . expresses a more intense emotion than ever in his newest pictures—tightly woven webs of paint applied in heavy streaks by weighted strings and sticks. . . . While the closely woven layers of different colored lines appear at first to represent impulsive snapping of all restrictive bonds, including form, it is apparent that there is a definite pattern and feeling in each canvas, and forms emerge and recede from the criss-crossing calligraphies.

ROBERT M. COATES (*New Yorker*, December 3)
Jackson Pollock . . . has been an artistic mystery since he came to general attention, five or six years ago. He paints in an odd abstract style, made up of overlapping swirls and skeins of brilliant color. Till now, there has been a suggestion of forceful, rhythmic movement about his work that, taken in conjunction with its deliberate avoidance of content, is curiously baffling. His new show may clarify things somewhat. The forcefulness is still there, but better controlled, as the color is less strident, and although he still avoids anything approaching the representational, the new work has a feeling of depth and a sense of stricter organization that add greatly to its appeal. The pieces are not titled, so I won't try to list them. They seem to me the best painting he has yet done.

December 16, 1949–February 5, 1950. Whitney Museum of American Art, New York.
ANNUAL EXHIBITION OF CONTEMPORARY AMERICAN PAINTING. 1 painting: *Number 14, 1949*.

HENRY MC BRIDE (*New York Sun*, December 23)
The annual show of American paintings at the Whitney Museum down on Eighth Street is largely abstract. . . . The note of advance is sounded at once in the entrance hall by Jackson Pollock. For the first time I looked with respect and sustained interest upon one of his pictures. Previous works by him which I had seen looked as though the paint had been flung at the canvas from a distance, not all of it making happy landings. Even the present one has a spattered technic, but the spattering is handsome and organized. . . . The effect it makes is that of a flat, war-shattered city, possibly Hiroshima, as seen from a great height in moonlight. There is sparkle to the color and hints of a ribbon of a river holding the glimpses of the city together. The composition looks well in the entrance hall and will be the most discussed picture in the show.

(*Time*, December 26)
The annual exhibition of contemporary U.S. art that opened in Manhattan's Whitney Museum last week bulged with duds. . . . Most of the pictures on the walls looked like more or less distorted reflections of each other. Jackson Pollock's non-objective snarl of tar and confetti, entitled *No. 14,* was matched by Willem DeKooning's equally fashionable and equally blank tangle of tar and snow called *Attic*. If their sort of painting represented the most vital force in contemporary U.S. art, as some critics had contended, art was in a bad way.

Jackson Pollock, East Hampton, 1949

Through the winter and early spring Jackson and Lee lived in Alfonso Ossorio's house on MacDougal Alley in New York. They were to stay here occasionally on future trips into the city.

In March Pollock finished a mural for the Geller House in Lawrence, Long Island, which had been designed by Marcel Breuer. This commission was secured through Breuer with the assistance of the architect Peter Blake.

In the same month Peggy Guggenheim wrote to Betty Parsons of her unsuccessful efforts to arrange a one-man show for Pollock in Paris.

On May 20 Pollock joined other avant-garde painters—later called the "Irascible Eighteen" in the press—in signing an open letter addressed to Roland L. Redmond, President of The Metropolitan Museum of Art, refusing to participate in a national juried exhibition of contemporary American painting scheduled for December, on the grounds that the museum's director, Francis Henry Taylor, "has publicly declared his contempt for modern painting," and that the "choice of jurors . . . does not warrant any hope that a just proportion of advanced art will be included."

The *New Yorker* of August 5 carried an interview with Jackson and Lee in "The Talk of the Town." Lee was quoted as saying that Jackson was using numbers as the titles of his recent paintings because they were neutral and made the viewer look at a painting for what it was —pure painting. Jackson went on to say:

> Abstract painting is abstract. It confronts you. There was a reviewer a while back who wrote that my pictures didn't have any beginning or any end. He didn't mean it as a compliment, but it was. It was a fine compliment.

In the same interview Pollock spoke of the past:

> I spent two years at the Art Students League. . . . Tom Benton was teaching there then, and he did a lot for me. He gave me the only formal instruction I ever had, he introduced me to Renaissance art, and he got me a job in the League cafeteria. I'm damn grateful to Tom. He drove his kind of realism at me so hard I bounced right into non-objective painting. I'm also grateful to the W.P.A., for keeping me alive during the thirties, and to Peggy Guggenheim. Peggy gave me my first show, in 1943. She gave me two more, and then she took off for Europe, and Lee and I came out here. We wanted to get away from the wear and tear. Besides, I had an underneath confidence that I could begin to live on my painting. I'd had some wonderful notices. Also, somebody had bought one of

my pictures. We lived a year on that picture, and a few clams I dug out of the bay with my toes. Since then things have been a little easier.

Pollock discussed modern art and his own method of painting in a taped interview with William Wright, an East Hampton neighbor who was planning a radio program (see pages 79–81).

p. 65 In the fall Hans Namuth made a film of Pollock in which he painted two works, one of which, on glass, became *Number 29, 1950*.

PARKER TYLER, "Jackson Pollock: The Infinite Labyrinth" (*Magazine of Art*, March)
In being so overwhelmingly non-geometrical, Pollock retires to a locus of remote control, placing the tool in the hand as much apart as possible from the surface to be painted. In regularly exiling the brush and not allowing any plastically used tool to convey medium to surface, the painter charges the distance between his agency and his work with as much *chance* as possible—in other words, the fluidity of the poured and scattered paint places maximum pressure against conscious design. And yet the design *is* conscious, the seemingly uncomposable, composed.

pp. 47, 102 June 3 [8?]–October 15. Venice. XXV BIENNALE. 3 paintings: *Number 1, 1948, Number 12, 1949, Number 23, 1949*. The exhibition in the U.S. Pavilion was divided into two parts, selected under the joint organization of the Art Foundation, New York; The Museum of Modern Art, New York; and The Cleveland Museum of Art. One half of the Pavilion was devoted to a retrospective exhibition of the work of John Marin. The other half showed several paintings by each of six younger artists. Three—Hyman Bloom, Lee Gatch, and Rico Lebrun—were chosen by Alfred M. Frankfurter, President of the Art Foundation and U.S. Commissioner for the *Biennale;* the other three—Gorky, de Kooning, and Pollock—were selected by Alfred Barr.

EMILY GENAUER (*New York Herald-Tribune*, May 28)
Visitors who enter [the U.S. Pavilion] to learn about the state of art in America will see (with the exception of a group of paintings by the distinguished octogenarian, John Marin) not one single painting by any of the artists who have been recognized by our leading museums, critics, collectors and connoisseurs as the most creative and accomplished talents in America. There will be no canvas by Franklin Watkins, or Stuart Davis, or Max Weber, or Yasuo Kuniyoshi, or Feininger, or Shahn, or Reginald Marsh. . . . All that visitors will find . . . will be several canvases each by that singular and ubiquitous sextet, Jackson Pollock, William de Kooning, Hyman Bloom, Arshile Gorky, Lee Gatch, and Rico LeBrun.

ALFRED H. BARR, JR. (*Art News*, Summer)
Considerably younger than Gorky and De Kooning, Jackson Pollock . . . has developed perhaps the most original art among the painters of his generation. Pollock uses no brush, but lays his canvas on the floor and trickles the fluid paint on it from above, his hand weaving the thin stream of color into a rhythmic, variegated labyrinth. The result provides an energetic adventure for the

ABOVE: Jackson and Lee Pollock in front of the studio, East Hampton, about 1950

BELOW: Pollock in the studio, East Hampton, about 1950

p. 101

eyes, a *luna park* full of fireworks, pitfalls, surprises and delights. Sometimes, as in his masterpiece, *Number 1, 1948,* the whirling vortex of lines develops a mysterious depth and glow of light, without however destroying the sense of picture surface which Pollock and all his companions seek to preserve as essential to their art.

DOUGLAS COOPER (*The Listener,* July 6)
The younger painters in this pavilion mostly imitate well-known Europeans, with a singular lack of conviction and competence though on a very large scale. One of them, however, Jackson Pollock, is a striking exception. He is undeniably an American phenomenon. Working without brushes, he spreads his canvas on the floor and dribbles the contents of paint-tubes on to it from above. The result is an elaborate if meaningless tangle of cordage and smears, abstract and shapeless, but, to quote Alfred Barr of the Museum of Modern Art, it is "an energetic adventure for the eyes." Personally, I think this is merely silly.

(*Time,* August 21)
U.S. painting did not seem to be making much of a hit abroad last week. At Venice's "Biennale," the U.S. pavilion (featuring the wild & woolly abstractions of Arshile Gorky and Jackson Pollock . . .) was getting silent treatment from the critics.

DAVID SYLVESTER (*Nation,* September 9)
Six other painters are represented in the American pavilion by five or fewer pictures apiece—Bloom, Gatch, Lebrun, Gorky, Pollock, and de Kooning. If this pavilion is indeed representative, American painting has fallen prey to a Germanic over-estimation of the importance of self-expression. . . . There is no echo at the Biennale of the quality in which America's greatness lies—its use of technology to make the most of nature. Yet such echoes do exist, in Lloyd Wright and Calder. The difference between Calder and Pollock or Gorky is that Calder does not compose merely in accordance with his private emotional needs, but with natural laws of gravity and equilibrium, since his constructions, in order to exist, have to function perfectly. He thereby reflects the essential genius of America—its capacity to make things work.

ALINE B. LOUCHHEIM (*New York Times,* September 10)
Is it true . . . that our art is getting the "silent treatment"? . . . Have Jackson Pollock's paintings really caused a kind of havoc in Europe? . . .

The answer to the questions . . . is "yes-and-no." Our art has not been given the "silent treatment." . . .

It would be accurate to report . . . simply that Europeans do not bother to give our pavilion very serious consideration. Marin has received passing praise. . . . Even the most intelligent critics . . . spent little time looking at Gorky and de Kooning. . . .

Pollock is a special case. . . . His detailed description of how he works (dripping paint, etc., on to canvas spread on the floor) has been assiduously translated and is grounds for violent arguments pro and con all abstract and automatic art.

June 16–September 11. Stedelijk Museum, Amsterdam. AMERIKA SCHILDERT. 2 paintings: *Number 11, 1948, Number 12, 1948.* Introductory text, in Dutch, by Bartlett H. Hayes, Jr.

In the penthouse of The Museum of Modern Art, New York, 1950; left to right—Edward Steichen, René d'Harnoncourt, John Marin, Andrew Carnduff Ritchie, Lee Gatch, Alfred M. Frankfurter, Willem de Kooning, and Jackson Pollock

p. 96

July 22–August 12/15. Ala Napoleonica (Museo Correr) in Piazza S. Marco, Venice. One-man show. 20 oils, 2 gouaches, 1 drawing: *Drawing* (1942), *The Moon-Woman, Two, Don Quixote, Circumcision, Bird Effort, Direction, The Water Bull* (lent by the Stedelijk Museum, Amsterdam), *The Dancers, Sounds in the Grass* [*Croaking Movement*], *Eyes in the Heat*, 2 gouaches (1946), *Full Fathom Five, Enchanted Forest, Vortex, Magic Lantern, Prism, Alchemy, Reflections of the Big Dipper* (lent by the Stedelijk Museum), *Earth Worms, Sea Change, Number 16, 1949*. With the exception of the two paintings she had given to the Stedelijk Museum, these works comprised all the Pollocks in Peggy Guggenheim's collection. Two catalogues were printed for the exhibition: the first gave the closing date as August 12, cited Le Tre Mani as sponsors of the exhibition, and contained introductory remarks by Miss Guggenheim and an essay, " 'Guazzabugli' di Jackson Pollock," by Bruno Alfieri; the second gave the closing date as August 15, and omitted both the Tre Mani sponsorship and Alfieri's article.

BRUNO ALFIERI, "Piccolo discorso sui quadri di Jackson Pollock" (*L'Arte Moderna* [?], n.d.)
Jackson Pollock's paintings represent absolutely nothing: no facts, no ideas, no geometrical forms.

Do not, therefore, be deceived by suggestive titles such as "Eyes in the Heat" or "Circumcision": these are phony titles, invented merely to distinguish the canvases and identify them rapidly. . . .

No picture is more thoroughly abstract than a picture by Pollock: abstract from everything. Therefore . . . no picture is more automatic, involuntary, surrealistic, introverted and pure than a picture by Pollock. I do not refer to André Breton's surrealism, which often develops into a literary phenomenon. . . . I refer to real surrealism, which is nothing but controlled impulse. . . .

It is easy to detect the following things in all of his paintings:
— chaos
— absolute lack of harmony
— complete lack of structural organization
— total absence of technique, however rudimentary
— once again, chaos. . . .

Pollock has broken all barriers between his picture and himself: his picture is the most immediate and spontaneous painting. . . .

Jackson Pollock is the modern painter who sits at the extreme apex of the most advanced and unprejudiced avant-garde of modern art. . . . Compared to Pollock, Picasso . . . who for some decades has troubled the sleep of his colleagues with the everlasting nightmare of his destructive undertakings, becomes a quiet conformist, a painter of the past.

The same issue of this magazine carried an Italian translation of Pollock's statement that had appeared in *Possibilities* (1947/48).

October 1950–May 1954. CALLIGRAPHIC AND GEOMETRIC: TWO RECENT LINEAR TENDENCIES IN AMERICAN PAINTING. 1 work: *Number 31, 1949;* withdrawn mid-tour (November 1953) and substituted by *Number 12, 1948.* An exhibition organized by the Department of Circulating Exhibitions of The Museum of Modern Art, New York, which traveled to 25 places in the United States.

p. 101

October 21–November [?]. Galleria d'Arte del Naviglio, Milan. One-man show. Whether this exhibition included all the Pollocks in Miss Guggenheim's collection, or only a selection, is not known.

October 23–November 11. Sidney Janis Gallery, New York. YOUNG PAINTERS IN U.S. & FRANCE. 1 painting: *Number 8, 1950.* The exhibition, directed by Leo Castelli, compared American and French painters: Gorky with Matta, Kline with Soulages, de Kooning with Dubuffet, Pollock with Lanskoy (*Heavenly Harvest*), Rothko with de Staël. The day before the exhibition closed there was an open meeting at the gallery, "Parallel Trends in Vanguard Art in the U.S. and France"; the discussion panel included Castelli, Nicolas Calas, Clement Greenberg, Frederick Kiesler, Andrew Carnduff Ritchie, Harold Rosenberg, and Theodore Brenson, moderator.

p. 113

November 10–December 31. Whitney Museum of American Art, New York, ANNUAL EXHIBITION OF CONTEMPORARY AMERICAN PAINTING. 1 painting: *Number 3, 1950.*

"Chaos, Damn It!" (*Time*, November 20). An article that continued the *Biennale* story: "Pollock followed his canvases to Italy, exhibited them in private galleries in Venice and Milan. Italian critics tended to shrug off his shows. Only one, brash young (23) Critic Bruno Alfieri of Venice took the bull by the horns." The remainder of the piece quoted the portions of Alfieri's article which spoke of chaos.

Pollock responded to the article with a telegram that was published in the December 11 issue of *Time*:

NO CHAOS DAMN IT. DAMNED BUSY PAINTING AS YOU CAN SEE BY MY SHOW COMING UP NOV. 28. I'VE NEVER BEEN TO EUROPE. THINK YOU LEFT OUT MOST EXCITING PART OF MR. ALFIERI'S PIECE.

pp. 8-9, 65, 105-9, 113

November 28–December 16. Betty Parsons Gallery, New York. One-man show. 32 paintings, all 1950. On canvas, titled respectively, *Number 1* [*Lavender Mist*], *2* [*Shadows*], *3, 4, 5, 6, 7, 8, 9, 10, 11, 12, 13, 14, 15, 16, 17, 18, 19, 20, 21, 22, 23, 24, 25, 26, 27, 28, 30* [*Autumn Rhythm*], *31* [*One*], *32;* on glass, *Number 29.*

R[OBERT] G[OODNOUGH] (*Art News,* December)
Jackson Pollock . . . the most highly publicized of the younger American abstractionists whose controversial reputation is beginning to grow abroad, has been deeply occupied with some enormous paintings this summer—the largest are 20 by 9 feet. *No. 100* [*sic*] of this series is done in great, open black rhythms that dance in disturbing degrees of intensity, ecstatically energizing the powerful image in an almost hypnotic way. His strength and personal understanding of the painter's means allow for rich experience that projects a highly individualized (yet easily communicable to the un-selfconscious observer) sense of vision that carries as well through to the smaller colorful paintings in which convergences of tensions rule. Pollock has found a discipline that releases tremendous emotive energy combined with a sensitive statement that, if to some overpowering, can not be absorbed in one viewing—one must return.

B[ELLE] K[RASNE] (*Art Digest,* December 1)
Those who go for the no-intellectual-strings-attached sort of decoration will go for this year's Jackson Pollock show, his richest and most exciting to date.

Scrawled with the crazy, whip-lashing calligraphy which is Pollock's special mark, items of billboard proportions are packed into one small room. The effect is dizzying. But this year, they come big, beautiful yet subtle. Space is limited; Pollock apparently isn't. Outsize areas are painted in dainty pinks and blues or peppered with color dots in a 20th-century version of pointillism. Brittle, brilliant enamels and glistening silver paint weave immensely complicated webs. Paint spreads into blobs or dries in embossed cords.

An ingenious departure, a Pollock on glass, is concocted of wire mesh patches, embedded bits of colored glass and string, and pebbles stuck in glue, dried to resemble nut crunch.

HOWARD DEVREE (*New York Times,* December 3)
More than ever before . . . it seems to me that Pollock's work is well over toward automatic writing

and that its content (not definite subject-matter but *content*) is almost negligible—that what one gets out of it one must first put there. It has been called "an energetic adventure for the eye," which it may well be. In fact, one of the huge and sprawling paintings strongly suggests a railroad map with lines wandering between black junctions or nexuses. . . . But isn't all this rather in the nature of the day-dreaming we have all done while staring at a wallpaper pattern and ourselves investing it with ideas? . . .

Without for an instant questioning Pollock's sincerity and plastic ability may we not ask: Is not the logical outcome of this type of painting a double escapism—escape from the discipline of art and the organization which turns pattern into design, and escape from any pronouncement on the breadth and profundity of human experience out of which art grows?

Unsigned review (*The Compass* [New York], December 3)
His best designs manage to achieve an amazing, unhackneyed, luminous surface decorativeness. The successful ones speak to the eye of dazzling mosaic texture, a whirlpool of furious movement, a rousing, reckless bravado. They are a complete surrender to the enchanting sensuousness of color and line as an art in itself.

This form of abstract art carries within it deadly limitations. By restricting itself so severely to an intense emotion through design and pattern, it creates designs for the eye to explore, but frustrates the mind. It seems to lead to a blind alley.

This is indicated in a number of small panels by Pollock which seem like chic refinements of his own more vigorous style. These panels are tame copies, seemingly designed to beguile less daring buyers. Here Pollock is at his weakest and least sincere. Significantly more and more silver and metallic paint substitutes for true color decoration.

This deterioration also applies to a construction on a glass panel, made with paint, pebbles, bits of colored glass and mesh wire. This object again exudes a chic, stylish, mildly shocking quality which might appeal to an advanced window decorator. Pollock has undeniable power and force. But where can he go from here—into denser, deeper creativity, or into slighter objects for the fashionable trade?

The exhibition was voted among the three outstanding one-man shows by the editorial staff of *Art News* (January 1951); Pollock ranked second, preceded by Marin and followed by Giacometti.

1951

Early in January Pollock wrote to Alfonso Ossorio in Europe:

Gorky's show opened yesterday—it's really impressive and wonderful to see an artist's development in one big show. More than 90 percent of the work I'd never seen before —he was on the beam the last few years of his life. The catalogue doesn't have enough reproductions in it, but will send you one anyway.

I found New York terribly depressing after my show—and nearly impossible—but am coming out of it now.

Later in the month he wrote again to Ossorio:

> I really hit an all time low—with depression and drinking—NYC is brutal. . . .
>
> Have you seen the Matisse church and designs or is that terribly far from Paris? Hans and Falkenberg are still working on the movie. . . .
>
> I hope this letter doesn't seem so damned down and out—because I have been making some drawings on Japanese paper—and feel good about them.

On February 9 and 10 Pollock was in Chicago to serve on the jury (with James Lechay, then visiting artist at the University of Iowa, and Max Weber) for the exhibition of "Momentum," a group of artists which, in opposition to certain discriminatory practices on the part of the Art Institute of Chicago, had been holding independent annual exhibitions since 1948. (MOMENTUM 1951 was held March 10–April 7, 1951, in Werner's Books, Inc., Chicago.)

At the end of February Pollock wrote Ossorio that "the concentration here is toward wall painting—for the moment." He was interested in creating murals and established friendships with a number of architects, among them Tony Smith, whom he had known early in the forties.

The May issue of *Art News* contained an article by Robert Goodnough, "Pollock Paints a Picture," with photographs by Hans Namuth, in which Pollock's methods of working were clearly set forth for the first time:

> At one end of the barn the floor is literally covered with large cans of enamel, aluminum and tube colors. . . . Three or four cans contain stubby paint brushes of various sizes. About the rest of the studio, on the floor and walls, are paintings in various stages of completion, many of enormous proportions. Here Pollock often sits for hours in deep contemplation of work in progress, his face forming rigid lines and often settling in a heavy frown. A Pollock painting is not born easily, but comes into being after weeks, often months of work and thought. At times he paints with feverish activity, or again with slow deliberation. . . .
>
> Pollock has developed a method that is unique and that, because of its newness, shocks many. He has found that what he has to say is best accomplished by laying the canvas on the floor, walking around it and applying the paint from all sides. The paint—usually enamel, which he finds more pliable—is applied by dipping a small house brush or stick or trowel into the can and then, by rapid movements of the wrist, arm and body, quickly allowing it to fall in weaving rhythms over the surface. The brush seldom touches the canvas, but is a means to let color drip or run in stringy forms that allow for the complexity of design necessary to the artist.

By early June the Pollocks were back in Springs. Both were painting. On June 7 Pollock wrote to Ossorio:

> Lee is doing some of her best painting—it has a freshness and bigness that she didn't get before—I think she will have a handsome show. I've had a period of drawing on canvas in black—with some of my early images coming thru—think the non-objectivists will find them disturbing—and the kids who think it simple to splash a Pollock out.

On June 14 the film of Pollock painting by Hans Namuth and Paul Falkenberg, with music by Morton Feldman and narration by Pollock, had its first public showing at The Museum of Modern Art, New York.

About this time Pollock began seriously to consider leaving the Betty Parsons Gallery.

During the summer Pollock prepared for fall shows in New York and Chicago. Early in August he wrote Ossorio: "This has been a very quiet summer—no parties hardly any beach—and a lot of work."

In September Pollock began an intensive biochemical treatment for his alcoholism. This continued until the fall of 1953 and required him to come into New York City somewhat regularly to see his physician.

THOMAS B. HESS, *Abstract Painting* (New York, 1951)
As the first of the group of New York abstractionists to become a public success, Pollock has had considerable influence on younger painters in his use of calligraphy and in his insistence on the absolutely spontaneous touch, as well as by his example of glorifying the creative act—a more dangerous concept for the inexperienced. And with such gratifying attentions have come several equally distasteful ones. When conservatives or Marxists wish to point to some real or fancied evil, they almost invariably hit at Pollock. The Soviet art critic and the one writing for *Time* magazine, both covering the 1950 *Biennale* exposition in Venice (which included Marin, Bloom, Gatch, Gorky and de Kooning as well as Pollock), were hunting, respectively, for some particularly horrifying evidence of bourgeois decadence, and for some un-American scrawling. Both found what they sought in Pollock. He is accused of being too fashionable and too obscure, the head of a coterie and minor eccentric, etc., etc. Thus true fame has come to him from his detractors, and his best publicity has been of the wrong kind.

January 19–February 26. Stedelijk Museum, Amsterdam. SURREALISME & ABSTRACTIE. KEUZE UIT DE VERZAMELING PEGGY GUGGENHEIM. 19 works. The exhibition then went to the Palais des Beaux-Arts, Brussels, where it was shown March 3–28 under the title, SURRÉALISME & ABSTRACTION. CHOIX DE LA COLLECTION PEGGY GUGGENHEIM. One catalogue was printed for both exhibitions, in Dutch and French.

p. 47

January 23–March 25. The Museum of Modern Art, New York. ABSTRACT PAINTING AND SCULPTURE IN AMERICA. 1 painting: *Number 1, 1948*. Exhibition directed by Andrew Carnduff Ritchie. Pollock was placed in the "Expressionist Biomorphic" category. (Almost all the data given in Pollock's biographical note in the catalogue are incorrect.)

February 27–March 18. Ueno Art Gallery, Tokyo. THIRD TOKYO INDEPENDENT ART EXHIBITION. 2 paintings: *Number 11, 1949, Number 7, 1950*.

p. 113

March 8–31. Galerie Nina Dausset, Paris. VÉHÉMENCES CONFRONTÉES. 1 painting: *Number 8, 1950*. "For the first time in France the confrontation of the most advanced American, Italian and French painters of to-day presented by Michel Tapié." Also included were Camille Bryen, Capogrossi, Hans Hartung, Willem de Kooning, Georges Mathieu, Jean-Paul Riopelle, Alfred Russell, and Wols.

March 17–May 6. Whitney Museum of American Art, New York. ANNUAL EXHIBITION OF CONTEMPORARY AMERICAN SCULPTURE, WATERCOLORS, AND DRAWINGS. 1 work: *Watercolor Number 1, 1951*.

Sculpture by Pollock in the exhibition, SCULPTURE BY PAINTERS, at the Peridot Gallery. Untitled. (1951). Chicken wire covered with colored drawings on Japanese paper, about 5 feet long. Made for the exhibition, the piece was mounted on a wooden door and shown on the floor. After the show Pollock took it to Springs and left it out of doors so that it was finally destroyed by the weather. The painting at the left is also by Pollock

March 27–April 21. Peridot Gallery, New York. SCULPTURE BY PAINTERS. 1 papier-mâché sculpture: Untitled. "The sculpture of nine painters describing some of their ideas with a different clarity." Others included were James Brooks, Arthur Drexler, Seymour Franks, Weldon Kees, Gabor Peterdi, Reginald Pollack, Alfred Russell, and Esteban Vicente.

April 15–May 15. Kunsthaus, Zurich. MODERNE KUNST AUS DER SAMMLUNG PEGGY GUGGENHEIM. 8 works. Introductory remarks in the catalogue by Max Bill. The same exhibition, somewhat reduced because of lack of space, that was shown in Amsterdam and Brussels, January–March.

May 21–June 10. 60 East 9th Street, New York City. 9TH STREET SHOW. 1 painting: *Number 1, 1949*. An exhibition organized by some of the charter members of "The Club" (Franz Kline, Corrado Marca-Relli, John Ferren) with the help of Leo Castelli, who chose the artists and installed the show. Sixty-one artists were listed on the announcement, which was designed by Kline.

June 4–August 30. University Gallery, University of Minnesota, Minneapolis. 40 AMERICAN PAINTERS, 1940–1950. 2 works: *Number 22, 1948, Number 12, 1950*. "The forty artists selected were thought by competent critics and other artists to have established a substantial place in the painting world of 1950 and who had been exhibited professionally ten years ago." Exhibition directed by H. H. Arnason.

June 26–July 8. Hilltop Theatre Art Room, Lutherville, Maryland. One-man show. 12 works: 2 of 1948, *Number 4, Number 11*; 8 of 1950, titled respectively, *Number 4, 6, 9, 11, 17, 19, 23, 24*; and 2 of 1951 *Number 2, Watercolor Number 1*.

September 6–30. Museum für Völkerkunde, West Berlin. Title of exhibition not known. 2 paintings: *Number 9, 1950, Number 2, 1951*. An exhibition of American paintings and prints from the eighteenth to the twentieth century presented as part of a cultural festival held under the auspices of the American, British, and French High Commissioners. The exhibition, selected by a countrywide committee of museum directors working under the auspices of the American Federation of Arts, was the first such showing in postwar Germany.

pp. 105, 107

October 2–27. The Arts Club of Chicago. BEN SHAHN—WILLEM DE KOONING—JACKSON POLLOCK. 7 paintings: *Number 1, 1949*, and 6 of 1950, titled respectively, *Number 1, 11, 19, 23, 27, 28*.

p. 99

October–December. Museu de Arte Moderna, São Paulo. I BIENAL. 1 painting: *Lucifer*. U.S. presentation, under the auspices of The Museum of Modern Art, New York, organized by a committee under the direction of Andrew Carnduff Ritchie.

November 8, 1951–January 6, 1952. Whitney Museum of American Art, New York. ANNUAL EXHIBITION OF CONTEMPORARY AMERICAN PAINTING. 1 painting: *Number 2, 1951*.

pp. 65, 117-18

November 26–December 15. Betty Parsons Gallery, New York. One-man show. 21 oils, watercolors, and drawings, all 1951. Oils, titled respectively, *Number 3, 6, 7, 9, 10, 11, 13,* pp. 114-15, 119 *14, 16, 17, 18, 19, 21, 23, 24, 25* [*Echo*]; watercolors and drawings, titled respectively, *Number 1, 10, 11, 14, 17*. Catalogue introduction by Alfonso Ossorio:

> The attention focused on his immediate qualities—the unconventional materials and method of working, the scale and immediate splendor of much of his work—has left largely untouched the forces that compel him to work in the manner that he does. Why the tension and complexity of line, the violently interwoven movement so closely knit as almost to induce the static quality of perpetual motion, the careful preservation of the picture's surface plane linked with an intricately rich interplay upon the canvas, the rupture with traditional compositional devices that produces, momentarily, the sense that the picture could be continued indefinitely in any direction?
>
> His painting confronts us with a visual concept organically evolved from a belief in the unity that underlies the phenomena among which we live. Void and solid, human action and inertia, are metamorphosed and refined into the energy that sustains them and is their common denominator. . . .
>
> New visions demand new techniques: Pollock's use of unexpected materials and scales are the direct result of his concepts and of the organic intensity with which he works, an intensity that involves, in its complete identification of the artist with his work, a denial of the accident.

The serigraphs by Pollock, printed by his brother Sanford McCoy, relate to paintings in this exhibition.

HOWARD DEVREE (*New York Times*, December 2)
The recent work . . . is with but one exception confined to black and white. There is furthermore, as indicated in his picture in the Whitney Annual, a hint of more conscious organization and suggestion of heads and figures in the swirl of black network. So far as these are intentionally representational elements they carry horrific suggestive power, turning the automatic emotional mazes into nightmarish expressionist visions as of half-glimpsed and enmeshed witches' sabbath, black mass and unholy groups of doomsday aspect, as if Rops or Munch had approached their themes nonobjectively. The new work seems to me to have gained immeasurably through this infiltration of conscious organization and to be getting away from what threatened to be a dead end.

F[AIRFIELD] P[ORTER] (*Art News*, December)
Jackson Pollock's new paintings represent a change in direction. On unsized duck, monochromatic black or brown enamel runs in pools which soak dull at the edges. . . . Because of their lack of color, these works are more like drawings than former Pollocks, but because of the new breadth . . . they are also more like paintings. . . . Figures now make an appearance—heads, faces, bodies, and they are reversible . . . either the white spaces count as the subject, or the blacks do . . . they are less decorations and more emotional expressions than his former work. In one way, Pollock is not ambitious; he does not try to solve difficult problems. Using accident as a ceramist might, he lets

the medium lead him into spontaneity, with all that this implies in terms of immediate communicability . . . he has not lost touch by repeating a manner to the point of staleness, though it must have been a temptation to re-do past successes.

J[AMES] F[ITZSIMMONS] (*Art Digest*, December 15)

In most of his new paintings Pollock has limited himself to black—thin, intensely black paint, twisting, trickling and swooping across raw canvas. The effect at times suggests a wall of densely intertwined vines pierced here and there by light. Where color is used it is a single shade of reddish-brown, with black still dominant. . . .

Now, from the webs and snares of black, faces and figures in ever changing combinations emerge, sometimes distinctly, sometimes only by suggestion. These faces seem to express many different emotions, often violently, as in caricature. The twisting fragmentary figures keep changing, too. . . .

By introducing associative elements into his work, Pollock has found his own way of dealing with human experience. In this sense, his new paintings possess an additional level of meaning and so transmit a more complex kind of experience than did his earlier work. It would seem that Pollock has confounded those who insisted he was up a blind alley.

CLEMENT GREENBERG (*Partisan Review*, January–February 1952)

Jackson Pollock's problem is never authenticity, but that of finding his means and bending it as far as possible toward the literalness of his emotion. Sometimes he overpowers the means but he rarely succumbs to it. His most recent show, at Parsons', reveals a turn but not a sharp change of direction; there is a kind of relaxation, but the outcome is a newer and loftier triumph. All black and white, like Kline's, and on unsized and unprimed canvas, his new pictures hint, as it were, at the innumerable unplayed cards in the artist's hand. And also, perhaps, at the large future still left to easel painting. . . .

Contrary to the impression of some of his friends, this writer does not take Pollock's art uncritically. I have at times pointed out what I believe are some of its shortcomings—notably, in respect to color. But the weight of the evidence still convinces me—after this last show more than ever—that Pollock is in a class by himself. Others may have greater gifts and maintain a more even level of success, but no one in this period realizes as much and as strongly and as truly. He does not give us samples of miraculous handwriting, he gives us achieved and monumental works of art, beyond accomplishedness, facility, or taste. Pictures "Fourteen" and "Twenty-five" in the recent show represent high classical art: not only the identification of form and feeling, but the acceptance and exploitation of the very circumstances of the medium of painting that limit such identification. If Pollock were a Frenchman, I feel sure that there would be no need by now to call attention to my own objectivity in praising him; people would already be calling him "*maître*" and speculating in his pictures. Here in this country the museum directors, the collectors, and the newspaper critics will go on for a long time—out of fear if not out of incompetence—refusing to believe that we have at last produced the best painter of a whole generation; and they will go on believing everything but their own eyes.

December 26, 1951–January 5, 1952. Sidney Janis Gallery, New York. AMERICAN VANGUARD ART FOR PARIS EXHIBITION. 2 paintings: *Number 9, 1949, Number 9, 1951.* The idea of the exhibition, organized with the help of Leo Castelli, was conceived by the Galerie de France, Paris, with the aim of presenting in Paris a selection of the most advanced painters in the United States. Also included were Josef Albers, Baziotes, James Brooks, de Kooning, Robert Goodnough, Gorky, Gottlieb, Guston, Hofmann, Kline, Matta, Loren MacIver, Motherwell, Russell, Reinhardt, Tobey, Tomlin, Tworkov, and Vicente.

1952

Pollock's contract with Betty Parsons expired the first day of the new year. He indicated his desire to remove his paintings from the gallery. On January 31 Mrs. Parsons wrote to him asking that he remain until May so that she might realize some business from his last show. In May, still finding himself in financial difficulties, he left the Parsons Gallery. After considering several offers he joined the Sidney Janis Gallery.

February 26–March 15. Galerie de France, Paris. REGARDS SUR LA PEINTURE AMÉRICAINE. 2 paintings: *Number 9, 1949*, *Number 9, 1951*. The Paris showing of the exhibition previously held at the Sidney Janis Gallery (December–January).

March 7–31. Studio Paul Facchetti, Paris. JACKSON POLLOCK 1948–1951. Exact number of works not known; among those shown were *Painting 1948*, *Number 17, 1949*, *Number 3, 1950*, *Number 5, 1950*, *Number 14, 1950*, *Number 16, 1950*, *Number 8, 1951*, *Number 19, 1951*,

p. 115 *Number 23, 1951* [*Frogman*]. Pollock's first one-man show in Paris. In addition to a translation of Alfonso Ossorio's text that had appeared in the catalogue of the 1951 Parsons Gallery exhibition, the catalogue contained an essay by Michel Tapié, who organized the exhibition:

p. 86

> From *The She-Wolf* of 1943 . . . to the recent works in black and white Jackson Pollock has climbed to first rank in the thrilling pictorial adventure of our time. Thanks to his towering personality he dominates and surpasses the limitations of his audience. Pollock's works of the first period, before his transition to non-figurative painting, were inspired by an intense expressionism that already gave him the stature of an authentic artist. . . .
>
> In the years 1945–46 when a new generation of non-figurative works blossomed forth in every corner of the world, Pollock passed from works with titled motifs to paintings with no subject, or with a subject so remote as to be undefined and illegible. But there was no break in this evolution, either in depth or on the surface. . . .
>
> As Pollock's experiments become more stringent he apparently imposes limits on himself in order to permit the dramatic element to become more intense. Still a great colorist, he abandons color and disciplines himself to explore the infinite possibilities of

Pollock's paintings installed in the exhibition, 15 AMERICANS, 1952; left to right—*Number 22, 1951, Number 3, 1951 [Image of Man], Number 29, 1950, Number 5, 1948*

black and white. This constraint upon his temperament acts like a springboard as he forces his informal calligraphy to its utmost limits in huge paintings that are among the most compelling phenomena of our time.

March 13–May 4. Whitney Museum of American Art, New York. ANNUAL EXHIBITION OF CONTEMPORARY AMERICAN SCULPTURE, WATERCOLORS, AND DRAWINGS. 1 watercolor: *Number 7, 1951.*

pp. 97, 108-9, 115

April 9–July 27. The Museum of Modern Art, New York. 15 AMERICANS. 8 paintings: *Number 5, 1948, Number 2, 1949, Number 7, 1950, Number 28, 1950, Number 29, 1950, Number 30, 1950 [Autumn Rhythm], Number 3, 1951 [Image of Man], Number 22, 1951.* Exhibition directed by Dorothy C. Miller. Catalogue essay on Pollock by Alfonso Ossorio is the introduction to the Parsons Gallery 1951 catalogue, with some slight alterations. Shortly after the exhibition opened Pollock wrote to Miss Miller:

> I want you to know what a wonderful job I think you did in hanging my room at the Museum. There was probably extra work for you (or was there?) in my staying away. At any rate I think it was wise of me. I wish I could give No. 7 a coat of glue sizing—it would take some of the wrinkles out of it. Perhaps when I'm in next time I can do it after museum hours. It wouldn't take more than ten minutes.

May 22–June 14. Metropolitan Art Gallery, Tokyo. THE FIRST INTERNATIONAL ART EXHIBITION. 1 painting: *Number 21, 1951.* Exhibition sponsored by the Mainichi Newspapers to provide Japanese artists, "who have been separated from the rest of the world for over twelve years," with a better knowledge of world art, and "as a gesture of our strong desire for peace"; shown July–September in Osaka, Nagoya, Fukuoka, and Kyoto. Among other

1952 [65]

Americans were Adolph Gottlieb, Yasuo Kuniyoshi, John Marin, Ben Shahn, Charles Sheeler, Theodoros Stamos, Max Weber.

October 16–December 14. Carnegie Institute, Pittsburgh. THE 1952 PITTSBURGH INTERNATIONAL EXHIBITION OF CONTEMPORARY PAINTING. 1 painting: *Number 27, 1951.*

November 10–29. Sidney Janis Gallery, New York. One-man show. 12 paintings, all 1952, titled respectively, *Number 1, 2* (A, B, C—3 paintings on one long strip of canvas), *3, 4, 5, 6, 7, 8, 9, 10* [*Convergence*], *11* [*Blue Poles*], *12.*

J[AMES] F[ITZSIMMONS] (*Art Digest,* November 15)
The news of the show is provided by three vast and quite magnificent new canvases . . . in which Pollock takes up from where he left off two years ago. In *No. 10* arabesques of bright orange and patches of watery blue, yellow and green are suspended in a capillary network of sinewy black lines. The use here of flux, of marbleized effects . . . is something new in Pollock. There is a feeling of landscape in *No. 11.* . . . In *No. 12* he abandons sumptuous tapestried textures. A tremendously exciting painting, it suggests the *fluids* of life, intermingling, expanding and undergoing gradual chemical change.

HOWARD DEVREE (*New York Times,* November 16)
Some of the paintings . . . range from four to eight feet in height and from thirteen to sixteen feet in length, jungle-like assemblies of the dripped line in brilliance of color that exceeds anything this pioneer of the method has yet attempted. And there are black-and-white examples, too. . . .
  Of the color mazes, "No. 12" . . . stands by itself. . . . Back of them—and seemingly back of this particular Pollock—there was an identifiable landscape source of inspiration with a use of deep space instead of obsession with mere surface. If this canvas similarly indicates a getting away from the confusion of means and ends which has been all too prevalent in nonobjective work it means also, in this reviewer's opinion, a long step forward.

R[OBERT] G[OODNOUGH] (*Art News,* December)
Last year's reduction to black and white pictures seems to be the starting point for most of the present work—some of these are held to black figure forms, a few colors are edged into others giving a sharp effect, but the majority develop out of black completely into color . . . glowing colors, creating new movements, melt and merge into a massive over-all effect that is both intimate and elusive. The very large paintings . . . make the gallery seethe with energy, yet a gentleness pervades that settles the pictures back to stillness. . . . One feels a struggle from the impassioned beginning to the final concise declaration. . . . When there is too much activity, strong bars of color act like bold guards to hold things back, as in *No. 11.*

S. LANE FAISON, JR. (*Nation,* December 13)
Number 11, one of the largest, is the finest I have yet seen. . . . Pollock's greatness, when applied to works like this, has not been exaggerated by his champions. On the other hand, I suspect he is incapable of producing a small work. The examples shown here and in previous exhibitions are mere fragments with little force of their own. . . .

Hans Namuth: *Portrait of Jackson Pollock.* 1952.
The Museum of Modern Art, New York, gift of
the photographer

A very recent trend, which I confidently predict will be called Pollock's puddle period, is visible in Number 12, another extremely large canvas. The power is there, but I find it dissipated in amorphous passages. In its emphasis on color areas, however fluidly bounded, it recalls some of the work of eight years ago, where a tighter mosaic was accomplished.

The exhibition was voted among the "ten best one-man shows of the year in New York galleries" by the editorial staff of *Art News* (January 1953); Pollock was second, preceded by Miró.

pp. 86, 93, 108–9, 114 November 17–30. Bennington College, Vermont. A RETROSPECTIVE SHOW OF THE PAINTINGS OF JACKSON POLLOCK. 8 paintings: *Pasiphaë, The Totem—Lesson II, The Key, Number 2, 1949, Number 9, 1950, Number 30, 1950, Number 2, 1951, Number 25, 1951*. First retrospective exhibition in America, organized and shared with Williams College. Catalogue commentary by Clement Greenberg. The exhibition was shown at Lawrence Art Museum, Williams College, Williamstown, Massachusetts, December 1–21.

1953

Pollock spent the year painting a series of major canvases in which he explored a variety of styles.

On October 29 Clyfford Still wrote to Pollock:

> Went up to Janis' gallery with Barney [Newman] the other day & took the liberty of pushing into the office to see some of the paintings you did this summer.
>
> What each work said, what its position, what each achieved you must know. But above all these details and intentions the great thing, to me, came through. It was that here a *man* had been at work, at the profoundest work a man can do, facing up to what he is and aspires to.
>
> I left the room with the gratitude & renewal of courage that always comes at such moments. This is just my way of saying thanks, & with the hope some of my work has brought some of the same to you.

March 1–April 12. University of Illinois, Urbana. CONTEMPORARY AMERICAN PAINTING AND SCULPTURE. 1 painting: *Number 5, 1952*.

p. 120 March 3–29. The Baltimore Museum of Art. ABSTRACT EXPRESSIONISTS. 2 paintings: *Number 9, 1952, Number 11, 1952* [*Blue Poles*]. Works selected by Vincent Melzac; catalogue introduction and notes by Thomas B. Hess. The four other painters in the exhibition were Philip Guston, Willem de Kooning, Jack Tworkov, Esteban Vicente. The exhibition then went to the Watkins Memorial Gallery of the American University in Washington, D.C.

April 9–May 29. Whitney Museum of American Art, New York. ANNUAL EXHIBITION OF CONTEMPORARY AMERICAN SCULPTURE, WATERCOLORS, AND DRAWINGS. 1 drawing: *Composition 1953* (oil and watercolor).

pp. 86, 121

April 24–June 8. Musée National d'Art Moderne, Paris. 12 PEINTRES ET SCULPTEURS AMÉRICAINES CONTEMPORAINES. 4 paintings: *The She-Wolf, Number 6, 1952, Number 10, 1952, Number 12, 1952*. Exhibition of nine painters and three sculptors organized and circulated by the International Program of The Museum of Modern Art. Selected by Andrew Carnduff Ritchie. The other artists included were Ivan Le Lorraine Albright, Stuart Davis, Arshile Gorky, Morris Graves, Edward Hopper, John Kane, John Marin, Ben Shahn, and Alexander Calder, Theodore Roszak, David Smith. The exhibition then traveled, July 1953–March 1954, to Zurich, Düsseldorf, Stockholm, Helsinki, and Oslo.

October 15–December 6. Whitney Museum of American Art, New York. ANNUAL EXHIBITION OF CONTEMPORARY AMERICAN PAINTING. 1 painting: *Number 5, 1952*.

Pollock was also included this year in the SECOND INTERNATIONAL CONTEMPORARY ART EXHIBITION (India), one of a series of exhibitions sponsored by the All-India Fine Arts and Crafts Society, New Delhi, designed to promote cultural understanding between India and foreign countries.

1954

Pollock painted few works this year.

---

p. 120

January 4–23. Sidney Janis Gallery, New York. 9 AMERICAN PAINTERS TODAY. 1 painting: *Blue Poles [Number 11, 1952]*. Also in the exhibition were Davis, Gorky, Hofmann, Kline, de Kooning, Rothko, Still, and Tobey. Each participant, "selected on the basis of stature and originality" was represented by "a single work to best point up the artist in his most creative aspect."

pp. 124-27, 130

February 1–27. Sidney Janis Gallery, New York. One-man show. 10 paintings, all 1953: *Ritual, Ocean Greyness, Easter and the Totem, Four Opposites, The Deep, Grayed Rainbow, Sleeping Effort, Portrait with a Dream* (title later became *Portrait and a Dream*), *Unformed Figure, Moon Vibrations*.

> EMILY GENAUER (*New York Herald-Tribune,* February 7)
> Although all . . . were executed during 1953, the earliest are done in his famous, controversial "drip" technique. I still find it and the pictures he made with it empty and pretentious wall decorations of varying degrees of tastefulness.

But there are just a few canvases at hand which indicate a new and promising approach. To begin with they're really painted, not dripped! In one of them, called "Sleeping Effort," are to be seen some plainly recognizable shapes—a long-billed bird, for example. . . . Actually, the two best works, called "The Deep" and "Easter and the Totem," are still devoid of identifiable objects, but richly communicative, none the less, of poetic mood and even specific theme. They are carefully controlled in composition and texture, subtly luminous in color. Others are notable for their restless, violent movement. Together they mark a real step forward in Pollock's development.

ROBERT M. COATES (*New Yorker*, February 20)
There is no gainsaying the power and authority that [Pollock] brings to his work. Nothing about his work is ever hesitant . . . and his faults, when they appear, are as definite as his virtues, of which they are frequently an extension. Thus his feeling for rhythmic design, which is one of his strongest features, often carries him over into mere repetitiousness . . . his fondness for the accidental . . . sometimes leads him into the development of only chance effects, so that the whole canvas seems capricious and a little trivial. He has a weakness, too, for the over-elaborate. . . .

All these faults are visible . . . in his current exhibition . . . but his virtues far outweigh them, and there are a number of new trends in his work to add greatly to the interest of the collection. In his last show, Pollock seemed to be moving . . . away from pure non-objectivity toward the at least partly representational, and this movement has been accelerated. . . . And though his famous "dribble" technique has not been wholly abandoned . . . it is generally used with more formal, compositional purpose, or as a background motif, instead of as an end in itself. In most . . . the paint is applied more conventionally. . . . If the show represents . . . a recapitulation by Pollock, a reassembling of his forces and a searching for new sources, it should lead to a considerable widening and strengthening of his powers.

JAMES FITZSIMMONS (*Arts & Architecture*, March)
Jackson Pollock is not a gentle man. He is an angry man. He is also one of the most original, powerful artists of his generation, as more and more people are beginning to realize. Some of us recognized his gifts from the start (or, more exactly, from the time he first began to make his famous "drip" paintings) but felt that his art was limited, that it excluded too many resources of the medium, too many levels of the mind and sensibility. Now, with his new paintings . . . Pollock has confounded his critics and bemused his admirers. For one thing, he has not repeated himself. And though he has introduced figurative elements into his work, he has not succumbed to that failure of nerve and imagination which has caused certain lesser talents to turn back to a banal near-naturalism—as if nothing had happened in art during the last fifty years. Instead he has enriched his art in every possible way (without, however, encumbering it with extrinsic ornament) and greatly extended its relevance. Not all of the new paintings come off but three or four are completely convincing, and two (*Ocean Greyness* and *Sleeping Effort*) are as fine as anything he has done. . . .

For this reviewer the exciting thing about Pollock's new paintings—the successful and unsuccessful alike—is the glimpse they afford into the metaphysical and psychological structure of things. For the powerful rhythmic alternations on which they are based are perhaps those of the life process itself. And, what is rare in abstract art, the complexity of their formal-technical characteristics corresponds to, and is justified by, that of their conceptual roots.

Pollock with his dogs, Gyp and Ahab, about 1955

T[HOMAS] B. H[ESS] (*Art News,* March)

Jackson Pollock's . . . 1953 paintings showed a return to some of his earlier statements and a new synthesis of their possibilities with his changing concept of activated space. . . . In his abstractions, Pollock still walks on the edge separating violence from decorativeness; in the new pictures containing figurative elements, the edge separates violence from sentimentality. That he passes so seldom beyond violence, and that he so consistently roots the image in its pictorial qualities, reaffirms one's belief in his international importance.

p. 47

March 2–31. Museum of the University City, Caracas, Venezuela. U.S. REPRESENTATION: TENTH INTER-AMERICAN CONFERENCE. 1 painting: *Number 1, 1948.* Exhibition sponsored by the Secretary General of the Organization of American States, who invited The Museum of Modern Art to select the United States section, which was directed by Margaret Miller.

March 17–April 18. Whitney Museum of American Art, New York. ANNUAL EXHIBITION OF CONTEMPORARY AMERICAN SCULPTURE, WATERCOLORS, AND DRAWINGS. 1 drawing: *Composition 1951* (oil on paper).

p. 126

May 12–July 25. The Solomon R. Guggenheim Museum, New York. YOUNGER AMERICAN PAINTERS: A SELECTION. 1 painting: *Ocean Greyness.*

1955

Pollock's period of inactivity continued. He told a close friend that he had not touched a brush for a year and a half because he wondered whether he was saying anything.

In July he took out a passport, which he never used.

During the summer he re-entered analysis, and until his death came into the city regularly for his sessions.

———

January 29–March 6. Kunsthalle, Bern. TENDANCES ACTUELLES. 11 paintings: *The Moon-Woman, Two, Eyes in the Heat, Sounds in the Grass [Croaking Movement], Enchanted Forest, Alchemy, Prism, Number 16, 1949, Number 14, 1950, Number 8, 1951, Number 19, 1951.* Catalogue preface by Michel Tapié. Among others in exhibition were Camille Bryen, Sam Francis, Georges Mathieu, Mark Tobey, and Wols.

pp. 47, 86

March 31–May 15. Musée National d'Art Moderne, Paris. 50 ANS D'ART AUX ÉTATS-UNIS. COLLECTIONS DU MUSEUM OF MODERN ART DE NEW YORK. 2 paintings: *The She-Wolf, Number 1, 1948.* The exhibition, a cross section of American works from the collections of The Museum of Modern Art, New York, supplemented by a few loans from its trustees and other patrons, inaugurated the "Salute to France," a series of cultural events presented in

Paris in the spring of 1955 at the request of the French government and under the auspices of the U.S. Embassy.

Following its presentation in Paris, the exhibition traveled (July 1955–August 1956) to six other countries and was shown in whole or in part in Zurich, Barcelona, Frankfurt, London, The Hague, Vienna, and Belgrade under the title "Modern Art in the United States: Selections from the Collections of the Museum of Modern Art, New York."

pp. 120, 130 May 11–August 7. Whitney Museum of American Art, New York. THE NEW DECADE. 3 paintings: *Number 2, 1951*, *Blue Poles* [*Number 11, 1952*], *The Deep*. Between October 1955 and May 1956 the exhibition circulated to San Francisco, Los Angeles, Colorado Springs, and St. Louis; *Blue Poles* and *The Deep* were shown only in New York.

October 13–December 18. Carnegie Institute, Pittsburgh. THE 1955 PITTSBURGH INTERNA-
p. 123 TIONAL OF CONTEMPORARY PAINTING. 1 painting: *Easter and the Totem*.

November 28–December 31. Sidney Janis Gallery, New York. 15 YEARS OF JACKSON
pp. 84, 86, 90, 93, 104, 108-9, 114, 121, 128 POLLOCK. 16 paintings: *The Flame, Masqued Image, The Magic Mirror, Pasiphaë, Gothic, The Totem–Lesson II, The Key, Eyes in the Heat, White Cockatoo* [*Number 24, 1948*], *Out of the Web* [*Number 7, 1949*], *Autumn Rhythm* [*Number 30, 1950*], *Echo* [*Number 25, 1951*], *Convergence* [*Number 10, 1952*], *Moon Vibrations, White Light, Search*.

STUART PRESTON (*New York Times*, December 4)
In these revolutionary paintings are demonstrated his progressive abandonment of forethought; the way he leaves things to chance, the ruthless steps he has taken to shatter the conventions of art and introduce, for the first time in art, raw and naked, the elemental and largely subconscious promptings of his creative nature.

No use looking for "beauty" or worrying about what socially relevant message is being communicated. Until psychology digs deeper into the workings of the creative act the spectator can only respond, in one way or another, to the gruff, turgid, sporadically vital reelings and writhings of Pollock's inner-directed art.

LEO STEINBERG (*Arts*, December)
Pollock's champions are a few critics and museum men, abstract painters who recognize in him a superior power, and, above all, those who know the man himself . . . [he] is a *cause célèbre* precisely because more than anyone he symbolizes a radical change in the social role of art. . . . The effect of [the] exhibition is entirely overwhelming. Questions as to the validity of Pollock's work . . . are simply blasted out of relevance by these manifestations of Herculean effort, this evidence of mortal struggle between the man and his art.

(*Time*, December 19)
Jackson Pollock, at 43 the bush-bearded heavyweight champion of abstract expressionism, shuffled into the ring at Manhattan's Sidney Janis Gallery, and flexed his muscles for the crowd with a retrospective show covering 15 years of his career. The exhibition stretched back to the time when

Passport photograph of Pollock, 1955

Pollock was imitating imitations of Picasso, reached a climax with the year 1948, when Pollock first conceived the idea of dripping and sloshing paint from buckets onto vast canvases laid flat on the floor. Once the canvases were hung upright, what gravity had accomplished came to look like the outpouring of Herculean energy. Pollock had invented a new kind of decoration, astonishingly vehement.

That was Pollock's one big contribution to the slosh-and-spatter school of postwar art, and friend and foe alike crowded the exhibition in tribute to the champ's prowess.

B. H. FRIEDMAN (*Art in America*, December)
Pollock's reality, his vision, is *freedom* which is one of those important words which has unfortunately become muddied in our time. . . . For Pollock the acceptance of freedom, the striving for fluidity, is and has been the supreme discipline. . . .

The techniques which Pollock has developed are the result of his need to express fluidity—energy and motion made visible. No image could better express this concept than that of liquid paint spilled on canvas. But remember that the use Pollock makes of the accidental is not itself accidental. He improvises, using the accidental, accepting the accidental (as one does, in nature), but not being dominated by it. . . .

When this article was discussed, Pollock said that he didn't want any direct quotes or revelations of his private life. He said he'd stand on his painting. The way he said it was rougher and firmer—and less "eloquent"—than Epstein's "I rest silent in my work." But the real difference was that Pollock meant what he said. He's never going to write an autobiography. He's painted it.

December 19, 1955–January 14, 1956. Betty Parsons Gallery, New York. TEN YEARS. I painting: *Night Dancer*. Catalogue commentary by Clement Greenberg.

1956

In May Andrew Ritchie wrote Pollock that The Museum of Modern Art was inaugurating a series of one-man shows called "Work in Progress," each of which would honor an artist in mid-career by showing up to 25 of his major works. The letter formally notified Pollock that the Museum planned to begin the series with an exhibition of his work.

In June Selden Rodman interviewed Pollock at East Hampton. He later published Pollock's remarks (*Conversations with Artists*, New York, 1957), including the following, concerning the "labeling" of his art:

I don't care for "abstract expressionism" . . . and it's certainly not "nonobjective," and not "nonrepresentational" either. I'm very representational some of the time, and a little all of the time. But when you're painting out of your unconscious, figures are bound to emerge. We're all of us influenced by Freud, I guess. I've been a Jungian for a long time . . . painting is a state of being. . . . Painting is self-discovery. Every good artist paints what he is.

1955-56 [73]

In July Lee Pollock sailed for a vacation in Europe. Pollock remained in the United States and continued in analysis.

At 10:15 P.M. on August 11, while going north on Fireplace Road in East Hampton, Pollock's car crashed into a clump of trees and overturned. He was killed instantly.

———————

"The Wild Ones" (*Time*, February 20). An article on avant-garde painting which cited Baziotes, Gorky, Gottlieb, Guston, de Kooning, Motherwell, Pollock, and Rothko. Among the remarks on Pollock:

p. 129

> Jackson Pollock's *Scent* is a heady specimen of what one worshiper calls his "personalized skywriting." More the product of brushwork than of Pollock's famed drip technique, it nevertheless aims to remind the observer of nothing except previous Pollocks, and quite succeeds in that modest design. All it says, in effect, is that Jack the Dripper, 44, still stands on his work.

April 27–June 10. The Newark Museum, New Jersey. ABSTRACT ART, 1910 TO TODAY.

p. 113   1 painting: *Number 8, 1950*.

June–September. Venice. XXVIII BIENNALE: AMERICAN ARTISTS PAINT THE CITY. 1 painting:

p. 121   *Convergence* [*Number 10, 1952*]. The Art Institute of Chicago was invited by The Museum of Modern Art, New York, to organize the presentation for the United States Pavilion. Exhibition assembled by Katharine Kuh. In the introduction to the catalogue of the United States representation, published by the Art Institute of Chicago, Mrs. Kuh wrote:

> It is Jackson Pollock who best expresses the tendency in canvas not consciously related to the city, but reminiscent of the bewildering emotions resulting from its complexity. Beneath the drip and tangle, the spot and dribble of a painting like *Convergence* . . . one senses the multi-colored rhythm of present-day America.

November 30. New York City. "An Evening for Jackson Pollock." A memorial meeting held by "The Club." The announced participants were James Brooks, Clement Greenberg, Reuben Kadish, Frederick Kiesler, Franz Kline, Willem de Kooning, and Corrado Marca-Relli, with Harold Rosenberg moderating. Barnett Newman also took part, and Mrs. Harold Rosenberg was one of those who spoke from the floor.

December 19, 1956–February 3, 1957. The Museum of Modern Art, New York. JACKSON POLLOCK. 35 paintings, 9 watercolors and drawings, covering the period 1938–1956. Exhibition directed by Sam Hunter.

ROBERT M. COATES (*New Yorker*, December 29)

Pollock . . . got his initial notice for his unconventional painting techniques, and to a great many people he is still chiefly known for them—which is unfortunate, for whatever his style he was obviously a devoted and deeply conscientious artist. . . . Pollock's . . . was the boldest break with convention. It led him to the edge of a whole new theory of design, in which form and structure would both be put aside in favor of a painting of pure rhythm, and though he never systematized that theory, there are signs that he was on the verge—in, for instance, "Cathedral" (with its august suggestion), the truly mazy "No. 4" of 1949, and the marchingly rhythmic "Blue Poles."

p. 42
p. 120

The show starts us off a couple of years before his "dribble" period . . . and it's not till "There Were Seven in Eight," dated 1945, that we come upon the first example of the style that was to become his trademark. Thereafter the show concentrates on pictures of this sort, and with good effect, for in aggregate they seem to gain in power, and the rooms devoted to these works really shimmer with color and movement . . . there are indications that as time went on Pollock was experimenting more and more . . . excising whole sections of paint to expose the bare canvas as in "Out of the Web," trying new materials, as in the glass-string-wire-shells-pebbles-and-paint "No. 29," and the like. Toward the end, apparently, he was trying to break the pattern entirely, and in such pieces as "Ocean Greyness," with its wavelike whorls of gray pigment; "Easter and the Totem," which represents a return to his earlier style, but with more elegance; and the rather too rigidly compartmented "Portrait and a Dream," one perceives an attempt to devise a new approach to his painting problems. These are powerful pictures, too, particularly the first two I have just named. But there's still something tentative about them, and it's too bad he didn't have time to work out his problems more fully.

p. 104
p. 65
pp. 123, 126

p. 124-25

1957–1959

September 22–December 31, 1957. São Paulo, Brazil. IV BIENAL: JACKSON POLLOCK 1912–1956. 34 paintings, 29 drawings and watercolors, ranging in date from the late thirties to 1956. Presented as part of the United States representation, organized under the auspices of the International Council at The Museum of Modern Art, New York. Selected by Frank O'Hara. The exhibition received a special *hors de concours* citation.

Between March 1958 and February 1959 the exhibition, accompanied by the Hans Namuth film, was circulated to Rome, Basel, Amsterdam, Hamburg, Berlin, London, and Paris.

DARIO MICACCHI (*L'Unità* [Rome], March 12, 1958. Daily, Communist Party organ)

Even in his style Pollock no longer possesses the courage of painting. He takes wherever he finds some affinity: Masson and Matta among the Europeans who migrated at the start of the second World War, and above all, from Arshile Gorky's abstract expressionist and surrealist tendencies. His technique diminishes and impoverishes rapidly as his pictorial language loses its ties and roots. . . . His painting knows no other rule but the one of chance. . . .

Pollock's own experience can teach one thing . . . and that is that this experience ends with itself and cannot have followers. . . . It is the conquest of a desert by a man who has turned off the light of reason in himself and in his work.

MARCELLO VENTUROLI (*Paese Sera* [Rome], March 13/14, 1958. Daily, pro-Communist)
Though we still believe that in great part we were right [to polemicize against abstract art], in the face of the retrospective exhibition of Pollock . . . we feel it our duty to modify our former position, and we do this with a great satisfaction, as an act of homage to art. . . . Yes, Pollock is a painter, he is an artist: we can only accept his magic and unequivocal results. Above all we must admit we were wrong in one of our tenets, and that is, we did not believe it possible today to paint or sculpt without a minimum of reference to exterior reality. Pollock, after Kandinsky, has succeeded, and with authority, in convincing us. . . .

p. 106

    The big painting *One* . . . is the most dramatic and tormented painting, not in the least casual or decorative. . . . It is the clear mirror of a temperament that unites, in a protest of anarchic origin, good and evil, harmonic and irrational forms with a universal result. This painting is a warning, a message, an irreducible and candid way of looking at the world.

GIOVANNI RUSSO (*Corriere d'Informazione* [Milan], March 26/27, 1958. Daily, independent)
For about three months in the artistic and literary circles in Rome there has been a particularly intensified battle between the two currents of representational and abstractionist artists among whom avant-garde painting is divided. This same battle has been raging with more or less intensity for a number of years, and with political implications. . . .

    This polemic was revived with special violence early this year when the Galleria d'Arte Moderna showed an exhibition of seventy-five paintings from the Guggenheim Museum in New York. The Communists immediately set up a howl. . . . A young critic of a pro-Communist evening paper, Marcello Venturoli, accused the director of the gallery, Palma Bucarelli, of having wished to force abstract art on the Italians. . . .

    In this heated atmosphere . . . there arrived the Pollock exhibition. . . . The Communists seemed about to carry the battle to Parliament when the little bombshell burst.

    That very same young critic who sparked the public fury wrote an article . . . in which he recognized his error. . . . His "recantation" provoked a kind of earthquake, the Communist cultural officials did not know what to do. . . . They decided to go see what kind of a thing these Pollock paintings were. . . .

    The little group of Communists murmured over the titles . . . they were perplexed but obliged to admire. . . .

    The Pollock exhibition . . . has been ignored by a large segment of the press but has aroused the attention of the Party organs, from the Christian Democrat *Popolo* down to the Communist *Umanita*. This Sunday hundreds of autos were parked by the Villa Giulia. . . . The lecture rooms were overflowing and could not hold the public.

FREEK VAN DEN BERG (*Het Vrije Volk* [Amsterdam], June 21, 1958. Daily, Socialist)
The importance of this painter lies especially in his unusual use of materials. He spreads his canvas on the floor—thus he is more a part of it (he said this himself) and makes puddles on it with paint that he scoops out of the can with sticks.

    Children also use their spoons to decorate their porridge with syrup. Pollock paints in the same way. . . .

    I cannot see Pollock's deep sensitivity and emotional lyricism. Instead I see Pollock . . . smashing a pot of paint and attempting to gain immortality with the contents.

WILL GROHMANN (*Tagesspiegel* [Berlin], September 7, 1958. Daily, independent)
Pollock . . . is more than the originator of the movement. Standing before his tremendous canvases . . . one does not think of styles and slogans but only of talent and singularity. . . . Here is reality, not of yesterday but of tomorrow . . . an exuberance of the continent, the ocean and the forests, the conceiving of an undiscovered world comparable to the time 300 years ago when the pioneers came to his country. And what refinement of pictorial conception; with what differentiation the single layers of consciousness are graded so that in the end the entire "reality" is there, called forth, not merely represented. For nothing is rendered as it is; everything is invented in the spirit of a natural and universal occurrence.

JOHN RUSSELL (*Sunday Times* [London], November 9, 1958. Weekly, independent Conservative)
[Pollock's] work is still more potent . . . than the things which have been said about it. Much of the gossip about him has, in fact, been misleading, in that the element of automatism has been stressed to a point at which Pollock's entire activity has been given the air of a stunt.

But what is likely to strike an attentive visitor to Whitechapel is something quite different: for these paintings, so often acclaimed for the apparently haphazard method of their execution, are in fact most carefully and conscientiously designed. Every accent is in place, and the great pounding rhythms which batter their way across the eighteen-foot canvases never for a moment get out of control.

JOHN BERGER (*New Statesman* [London], November 22, 1958. Weekly, independent Socialist)
The Pollock exhibition . . . certainly reveals that he was highly talented. . . . We have heard the legend of Pollock's way of working. . . . How surprising it is then to see that he was, in fact, a most fastidious, sensitive and "charming" craftsman. . . .

All his best canvases here are large. One stands in front of them and they fill one's field of vision: great walls of silver, pink, new gold, pale blue nebulae seen through dense skeins of swift dark or light lines. . . . They are designed as continuous surface patterns which are perfectly unified without the use of any obvious repeating motif. Nevertheless their colour, their consistency of gesture, the balance of their tonal weights all testify to a natural painter's talent, and . . . also to the fact that Pollock's method of working allowed him in relation to what he wanted to do, as much control as, say, the Impressionist method allowed the Impressionists.

Pollock, then, was unusually talented. . . . But can one leave the matter there? . . .

I believe that Pollock imaginatively, subjectively, isolated himself. . . . His paintings are like pictures painted on the inside walls of his mind. . . .

Given freedom and contact, he condemned himself to solitary confinement. . . . Possessing memories and countless references to the outside world, he tried to lose them. And having jettisoned everything he could, he tried to preserve only his consciousness of what happened at the moment of the act of painting.

If he had not been talented this would not be clear; instead one would simply dismiss his work as incompetent, bogus, irrelevant. As it is, Jackson Pollock's talent did make his work relevant. Through it one can see the disintegration of our culture, for naturally what I have described was not a fully conscious and deliberate personal policy; it was the consequence of his living by and subscribing to all our profound illusions about such things as the role of the individual, the nature of history, the function of morality.

DENYS SUTTON (*Financial Times* [London], November 25, 1958. Weekly, independent)
Pollock's art . . . is extraordinarily alert and positive. . . . Even if some of the explanations of his work may prove hard to swallow, its impact in its own right should appeal to all who delight in rich and emotive colour.

His painting can be . . . quite simply enjoyed as the introduction to an imaginative and spirited world; that this world happens to be largely a private one or rather based on the artist's own vision of colours and forms ought not to prevent us from sharing in its qualities. . . .

He was certainly more than a hit or miss painter who sloshed his paint about without awareness of the consequences . . . as the film of him at work demonstrates he was highly concentrated when he set about painting; he was on the hunt for that arrangement which would answer to the image which lay within his mind and which his hand (as the instrument of his conceptual processes) so patently directed. . . .

Above all one feels that his painting was influenced by his environment and his vast swirling compositions . . . express something of the energy and size of the U. S. . . .

He was a radical painter—as his compositions or those wonderfully whip lash drawings which bite into the surface with a sharp intensity . . . attest—but also, he belonged to a tradition. He was a traditionalist . . . because in the last analysis we are made aware of the potentialities of life itself; we are moved up a peg or so, not taken down.

In Basel, Berlin, and Paris the retrospective exhibition was shown in conjunction with THE NEW AMERICAN PAINTING, an exhibition selected by Dorothy C. Miller which toured eight European cities (Milan, Madrid, Amsterdam, Brussels, and London, in addition to the three mentioned) from April 1958 to March 1959 under the auspices of the International Council at The Museum of Modern Art and on its return was shown May 28–September 8, 1959 at The Museum of Modern Art, New York. Pollock was represented by four paintings: *Number 8, 1949, Number 26, 1951, Number 27, 1951, Number 12, 1952.*

July 11–October 11, 1959. Museum Fridericianum, Kassel. DOCUMENTA II. 16 paintings. Assembled as a one-man show at the request of the German exhibition committee as a special section of the U.S. participation organized by the International Program of The Museum of Modern Art, and shown with corresponding memorial exhibitions of two other artists who had died during the fifties, Wols of Germany and Nicolas de Staël of France.

1961–1964

Between June 1961 and February 1964 one-man shows drawn from the collection of Lee Krasner Pollock were exhibited in London, Rome, Milan, Düsseldorf, Zurich, Stockholm, Lund (Sweden), Copenhagen, and New York. The catalogue for most of these exhibitions contained an Introduction and notes by Lawrence Alloway.

In January 1964 ten examples of Pollock's work of the thirties were shown in an exhibition at the Griffin Gallery in New York.

An Interview with Jackson Pollock

Taped by William Wright in the summer of 1950 for presentation on the Sag Harbor radio station, but never used.

Mr. Pollock, in your opinion, what is the meaning of modern art?

Modern art to me is nothing more than the expression of contemporary aims of the age that we're living in.

Did the classical artists have any means of expressing their age?

Yes, they did it very well. All cultures have had means and techniques of expressing their immediate aims—the Chinese, the Renaissance, all cultures. The thing that interests me is that today painters do not have to go to a subject matter outside of themselves. Most modern painters work from a different source. They work from within.

Would you say that the modern artist has more or less isolated the quality which made the classical works of art valuable, that he's isolated it and uses it in a purer form?

Ah—the good ones have, yes.

Mr. Pollock, there's been a good deal of controversy and a great many comments have been made regarding your method of painting. Is there something you'd like to tell us about that?

My opinion is that new needs need new techniques. And the modern artists have found new ways and new means of making their statements. It seems to me that the modern painter cannot express this age, the airplane, the atom bomb, the radio, in the old forms of the Renaissance or of any other past culture. Each age finds its own technique.

Which would also mean that the layman and the critic would have to develop their ability to interpret the new techniques.

Yes—that always somehow follows. I mean, the strangeness will wear off and I think we will discover the deeper meanings in modern art.

I suppose every time you are approached by a layman they ask you how they should look at a Pollock painting, or any other modern painting—what they look for—how do they learn to appreciate modern art?

I think they should not look for, but look passively—and try to receive what the painting has to offer and not bring a subject matter or preconceived idea of what they are to be looking for.

Would it be true to say that the artist is painting from the unconscious, and the—canvas must act as the unconscious of the person who views it?

The unconscious is a very important side of modern art and I think the unconscious drives do mean a lot in looking at paintings.

Then deliberately looking for any known meaning or object in an abstract painting would distract you immediately from ever appreciating it as you should?

I think it should be enjoyed just as music is enjoyed—after a while you may like it or you may not. But—it doesn't seem to be too serious. I like some flowers and others, other flowers I don't like. I think at least it gives—I think at least give it a chance.

ABOVE: *Going West.* (1934–35). Oil on gesso ground on composition board, 15⅛ x 20⅞ inches. Collection Thomas Hart Benton, Kansas City, Missouri

RIGHT: *The Covered Wagon.* (1934). Oil on gesso ground on composition board, 10⅛ x 13 inches. Estate of the artist

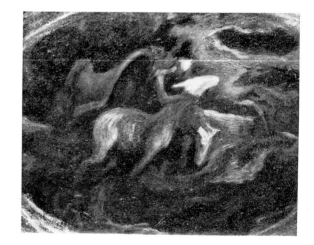

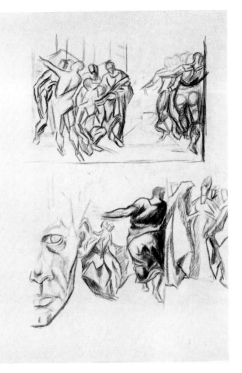

ABOVE LEFT: Studies after El Greco's *Healing of the Blind Man* and *Cleansing of the Temple*. Colored pencil, pencil, 17⅞ x 11⅞ inches. Estate of the artist

ABOVE RIGHT: Self-Portrait with Studies after El Greco's *Healing of the Blind Man*, *Holy Family*, and *Betrothal of the Virgin*. Colored pencil, pencil, 17⅞ x 11⅞ inches. Estate of the artist

RIGHT: *Figure in a Landscape*. (1938). Crayon, pencil, 11¼ x 14⅜ inches. Estate of the artist

ABOVE: *The Flame*. (1937?). Oil on canvas, mounted on composition board, 20⅛ x 30 inches. Estate of the artist

RIGHT: *Figures in a Landscape*. (1936?). Oil on canvas, 10¾ x 11⅞ inches. Estate of the artist

RIGHT: Sheet of Studies with a Bull. (1941). Pen and ink, 17⅞ x 13⅞ inches. Estate of the artist

FAR RIGHT: Sheet of Studies with Heads. (1941). Watercolor, pencil, crayon, pen and ink, 17⅞ x 13⅞ inches. Collection Joan and Lester Avnet, New York

BELOW LEFT: Studies. (1939–40). Colored pencil, crayon, pen and ink, 14 x 11 inches. Collection Dr. Joseph L. Henderson, San Francisco

BELOW CENTER: Study. (1941). Watercolor, pastel, pencil, brush, pen and ink, 13 x 10¼ inches. Collection Joan and Lester Avnet, New York

BELOW RIGHT: Studies. (1939–40). Colored pencil, pencil, crayon, brush and colored ink, pen and black ink, 14 x 11 inches. Collection Dr. Joseph L. Henderson, San Francisco

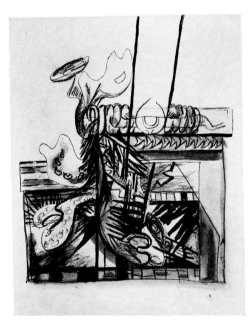

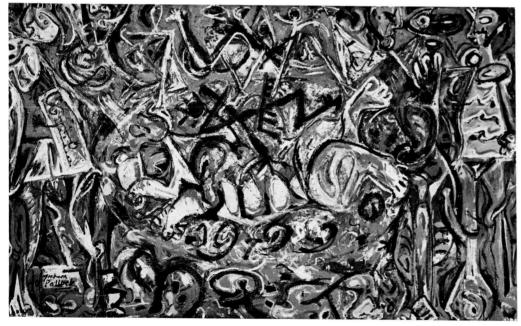

OPPOSITE ABOVE: *The She-Wolf.* 1943. Oil on canvas, 41⅞ x 67 inches. The Museum of Modern Art, New York

OPPOSITE BELOW: *Pasiphaë.* (1943). Oil on canvas, 4 feet 8 inches x 8 feet. Estate of the artist

BELOW: Untitled. (1943). Collage of colored papers with brush, pen and ink, crayon, colored pencil brushed with water, 15½ x 13⅝ inches. Collection Mr. and Mrs. Frederick R. Weisman, Beverly Hills, California

RIGHT: *Male and Female.* (1942). Oil on canvas, 73 x 49 inches. Collection Mrs. H. Gates Lloyd, Haverford, Pennsylvania

ABOVE: *The Guardians of the Secret.* 1943. Oil on canvas, $48\frac{3}{8}$ x $75\frac{1}{4}$ inches. San Francisco Museum of Art, Albert M. Bender Bequest Fund

RIGHT: Untitled. 1943. Gouache, 23 x $29\frac{1}{8}$ inches. Collection Mr. and Mrs. Davidson Taylor, New York

LEFT: *Portrait of H. M.* (1945). Oil on canvas, $36\frac{1}{8}$ x $43\frac{1}{8}$ inches. School of Art, The University of Iowa, Iowa City, gift of Peggy Guggenheim

BELOW LEFT: Untitled. (1943). Brush, pen and ink, colored pencil brushed with water, $18\frac{3}{4}$ x $24\frac{3}{4}$ inches. Estate of the artist

BELOW RIGHT: Untitled. (1943). Brush, pen and ink, colored pencil brushed with water, $18\frac{3}{4}$ x $24\frac{3}{4}$ inches. Collection Mr. and Mrs. Bernard J. Reis, New York

BELOW: *Gothic.* 1944. Oil and enamel on canvas, 84⅝ x 56 inches. Estate of the artist

RIGHT: *Mural.* 1943. Oil on canvas, 7 feet 11¾ inches x 19 feet 9½ inches. School of Art, The University of Iowa, Iowa City, gift of Peggy Guggenheim

[90]

OPPOSITE LEFT: *Night Ceremony*. (1944). Oil and enamel on canvas, 72 x 43⅛ inches. Collection Mr. and Mrs. Bernard J. Reis, New York

OPPOSITE RIGHT: *The Troubled Queen*. (1945). Oil and enamel on canvas, 74 x 43½ inches. Collection Mr. and Mrs. Stephen Hahn, New York

RIGHT: *The Totem, Lesson II*. 1945. Oil on canvas, 72 x 60 inches. Estate of the artist

ABOVE LEFT: *Blue (Moby Dick)*. (1946). Gouache and ink on composition board, 18¾ x 23⅞ inches. Ohara Art Museum, Kurashiki City, Okayama Prefecture, Japan

BELOW LEFT: *Red*. 1946. Gouache on composition board, 18⅜ x 23¼ inches. Collection Mr. and Mrs. Charles H. Carpenter, Jr., New Canaan, Connecticut

OPPOSITE

ABOVE LEFT: Untitled. 1944. Brush, spatter, pen and black and colored inks, 18¾ x 24¾ inches. The Art Institute of Chicago

ABOVE RIGHT: Untitled. (1944?). Brush, pen and black and colored inks, gouache, pastel, wash, sgraffito, 18¾ x 24¾ inches. Collection Mr. and Mrs. Alexander Liberman, New York

BELOW LEFT: Untitled. (1946). Pen and black and colored inks, pastel, gouache, wash, 22½ x 30⅞ inches. Collection Dwight Ripley, Greenport, New York

BELOW RIGHT: Untitled. (1946). Brush, pen and black and colored inks, pastel, gouache, wash, 22½ x 30⅝ inches. Collection Dwight Ripley, Greenport, New York

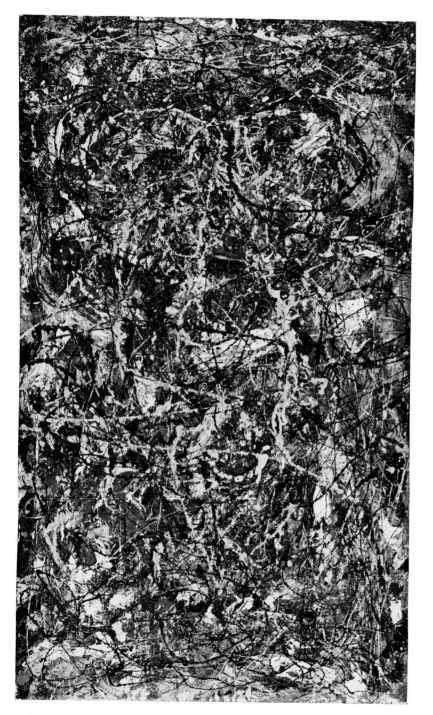

[96]

OPPOSITE: *Full Fathom Five*. 1947. Oil on canvas
with nails, tacks, buttons, keys, coins, cigarettes,
matches, etc., $50\frac{7}{8}$ x $30\frac{1}{8}$ inches. The Museum
of Modern Art, New York, gift of Peggy
Guggenheim

RIGHT: *Number 5, 1948*. Oil, enamel, and alumi-
num paint on composition board, 8 x 4 feet.
Collection Alfonso A. Ossorio and Edward F.
Dragon, East Hampton, New York

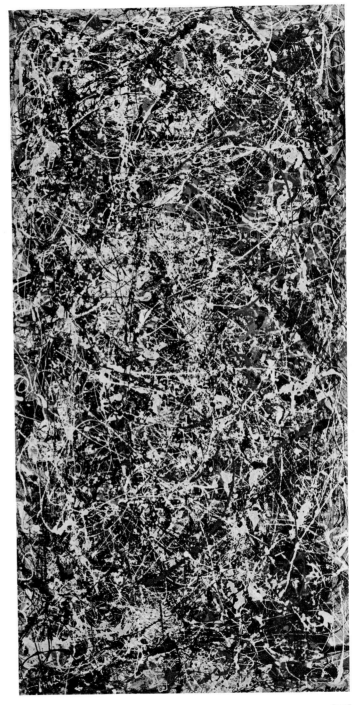

ABOVE: *Summertime* (*Number 9, 1948*). Oil and enamel on canvas, $33\frac{1}{4}$ inches x 18 feet 2 inches. Estate of the artist

BELOW: *Arabesque* (*Number 13, 1948*). Oil and enamel on canvas, $37\frac{1}{4}$ inches x 9 feet $8\frac{1}{2}$ inches. Collection Richard Brown Baker, New York

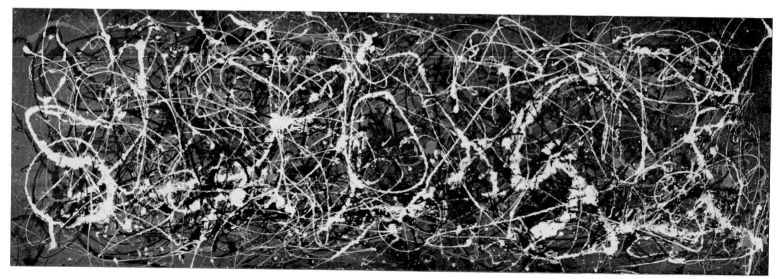

ABOVE: Untitled. 1948. Oil and enamel on metal, diameter 23⅛ inches. Collection Mr. and Mrs. Willard Gidwitz, Highland Park, Illinois

BELOW: *Number 12, 1948 (Yellow, Gray, Black)*. Enamel on wet gesso, 22½ x 30⅝ inches. Collection Mrs. Betty Parsons, New York

ABOVE: *Number 14, 1948 (Gray)*. Enamel on wet gesso, 22¾ x 31 inches. Collection Miss Katharine Ordway, Weston, Connecticut

BELOW: Untitled. 1948. Collage of paper with oil, enamel on wet gesso, 22⅛ x 30⅝ inches. Collection Mr. and Mrs. G. H. Petersen, New York

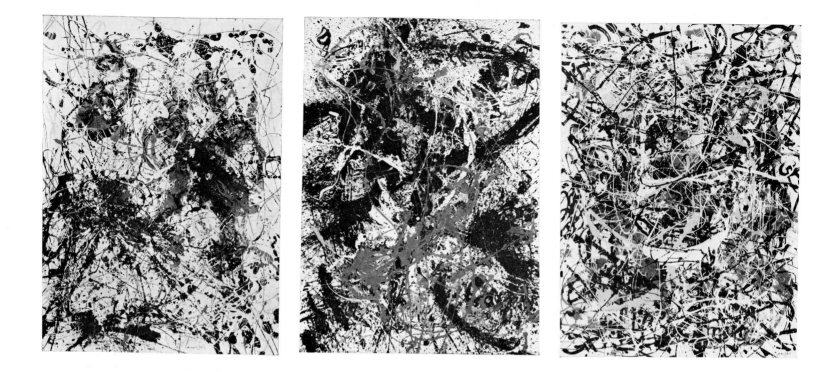

LEFT: *Number 12, 1949*. Enamel on paper, mounted on composition board, 31 x 22½ inches. The Museum of Modern Art, New York, gift of Edgar Kaufmann, Jr.

CENTER: *Number 15, 1949*. Enamel, aluminum paint on gesso ground on paper, mounted on composition board, 31 x 22⅜ inches. Collection Miss Priscilla Peck, New York

RIGHT: *Number 19, 1949*. Enamel on parchment, mounted on composition board, 31 x 22⅝ inches. Collection Dr. and Mrs. Israel Rosen, Baltimore

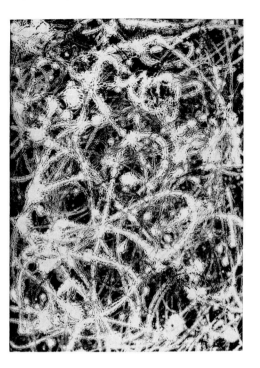

ABOVE LEFT: *Birds of Paradise* (*Number 30, 1949*).
Enamel, aluminum paint on paper, mounted on
composition board, 30¾ x 22½ inches. Collection Dr. and Mrs. David Abrahamsen, New York

ABOVE RIGHT: *White on Black*. 1949. Oil on canvas,
24⅛ x 17¼ inches. Sidney Janis Gallery, New
York

RIGHT: *Green Silver*. (1949). Enamel, aluminum
paint on paper, mounted on canvas, 22⅞ x 30⅞
inches. Collection Mr. and Mrs. Joseph Slifka,
New York

OPPOSITE: *Out of the Web (Number 7, 1949)*. Oil and enamel on composition board, cut out, 4 x 8 feet. Staatsgalerie Stuttgart

ABOVE RIGHT: *Number 27, 1950*. Oil, enamel, and aluminum paint on canvas, 4 feet 1 inch x 8 feet 10 inches. Whitney Museum of American Art, New York

BELOW RIGHT: *Number 8, 1949*. Oil, enamel, and aluminum paint on canvas, $34\frac{1}{8}$ x $71\frac{1}{4}$ inches. Collection Mr. and Mrs. Roy R. Neuberger, New York

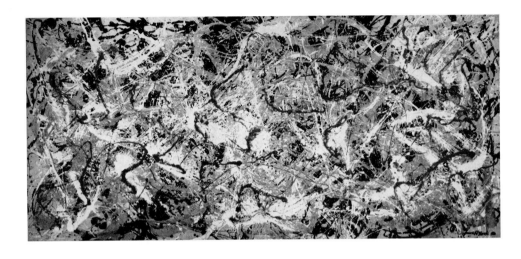

ABOVE: *One* (*Number 31, 1950*). Oil and enamel on canvas, 8 feet 10 inches x 17 feet 5 inches. Collection Mr. and Mrs. Ben Heller, New York

OPPOSITE: *Lavender Mist* (*Number 1, 1950*). Oil, enamel, and aluminum paint on canvas, 7 feet 3 inches x 9 feet 10 inches. Collection Alfonso A. Ossorio and Edward F. Dragon, East Hampton, New York

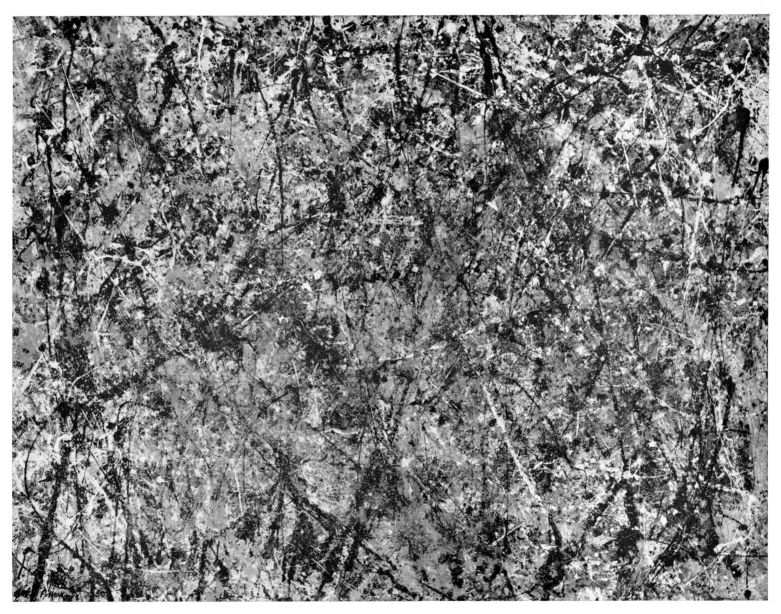

[107]

Autumn Rhythm (*Number 30, 1950*). Oil and enamel on canvas, 8 feet 10½ inches x 17 feet 8 inches. The Metropolitan Museum of Art, New York, George A. Hearn Fund, 1957

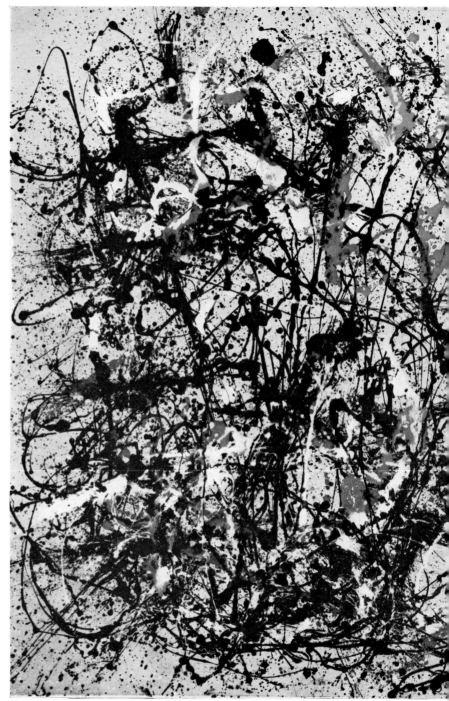

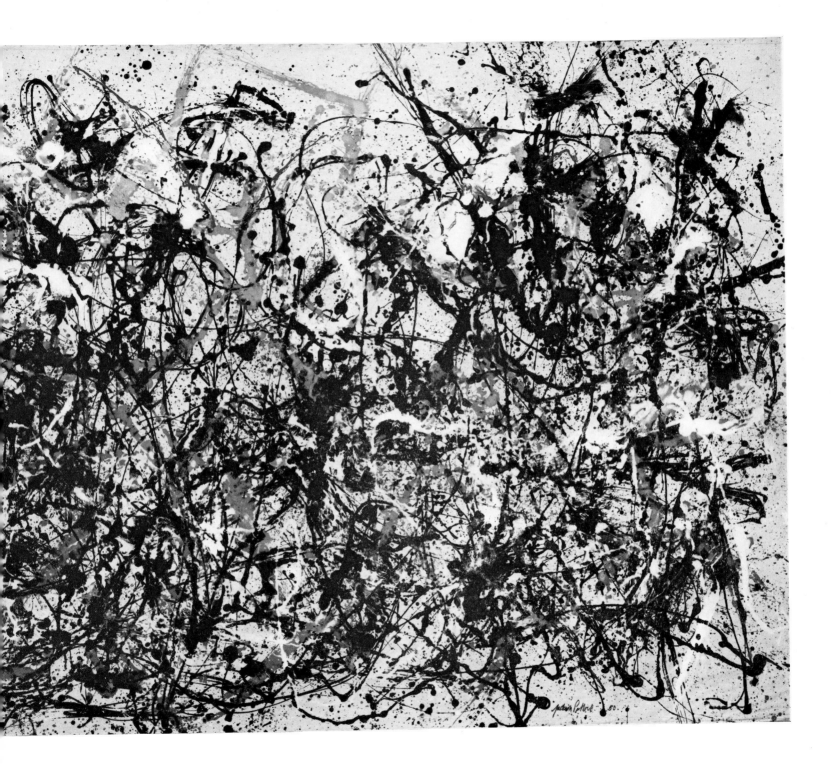

ABOVE: Untitled. 1950. Oil, enamel, and aluminum paint on canvas, 36⅝ x 25⅝ inches. Collection N. Richard Miller, Philadelphia

OPPOSITE: *Mural.* 1950. Oil, enamel, and aluminum paint on canvas, mounted on wood, 6 x 8 feet. Collection William Rubin, New York

[110]

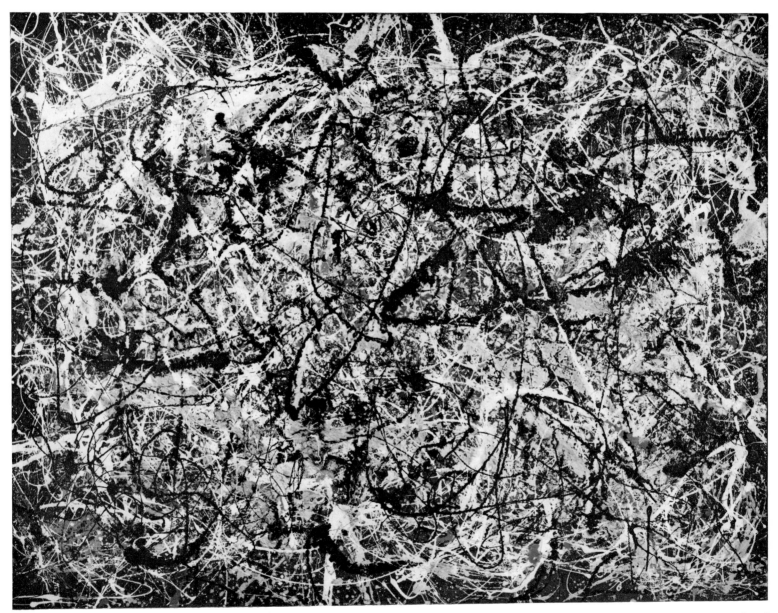

[111]

OPPOSITE LEFT: Untitled. (1951). Watercolor, ink on rice paper, 24¼ x 34 inches. Estate of the artist

OPPOSITE RIGHT: Untitled. 1951. Watercolor, ink on rice paper, 24½ x 34 inches. Collection Mr. and Mrs. B. H. Friedman, New York

RIGHT: *Number 8, 1950*. Oil, enamel, and aluminum paint on canvas, mounted on composition board, 56⅛ x 39 inches. Collection Mrs. Enid A. Haupt, New York

OPPOSITE: *Echo (Number 25, 1951)*. Enamel on canvas, 7 feet 8 inches x 7 feet 1¾ inches. Collection Mr. and Mrs. Ben Heller, New York

LEFT: *Number 3, 1951 (Image of Man)*. Enamel on canvas, 56 x 24 inches. Collection Robert U. Ossorio, New York

BELOW: *Number 23, 1951 (Frogman)*. Enamel on canvas, 58⅝ x 47¼ inches. Martha Jackson Gallery, New York

[116]

OPPOSITE: *Number 7, 1952*. Enamel on canvas, 53⅛ x 40 inches. Estate of the artist

RIGHT: *Number 10, 1951*. Enamel on canvas, mounted on composition board, 59⅞ x 29 inches. Collection Alfonso A. Ossorio and Edward F. Dragon, East Hampton, New York

ABOVE: *Number 11, 1951*. Enamel on canvas, 4 feet 9½ inches x 11 feet 6 inches. Estate of the artist

OPPOSITE: *Number 14, 1951*. Oil on canvas, 4 feet 9⅝ inches x 8 feet 10 inches. Estate of the artist

[119]

ABOVE: *Blue Poles* (*Number 11, 1952*). (Subsequently inscribed 1953). Enamel and aluminum paint with glass on canvas, 6 feet 11 inches x 16 feet. Collection Mr. and Mrs. Ben Heller, New York

OPPOSITE: *Convergence* (*Number 10, 1952*). Enamel on canvas, 7 feet 9½ inches x 13 feet. Albright-Knox Art Gallery, Buffalo, New York, gift of Seymour H. Knox

[120]

[121]

OPPOSITE ABOVE: *Number 3, 1952*. Enamel on canvas, 55⅞ x 66 inches. Collection Alfonso A. Ossorio and Edward F. Dragon, East Hampton, New York

OPPOSITE BELOW: Untitled. (1953–54). Brush and black and colored inks on Howell paper, 15¾ x 20½ inches. The Museum of Modern Art, New York, gift of Mr. and Mrs. Ira Haupt

RIGHT: *Easter and the Totem*. 1953. Oil on canvas, 82¼ x 58 inches. Estate of the artist

Portrait and a Dream. 1953. Enamel on canvas, 4 feet 10¼ inches x 11 feet 2½ inches. Acquired for the Dallas Museum of Fine Arts by Mr. and Mrs. Algur Hurtle Meadows

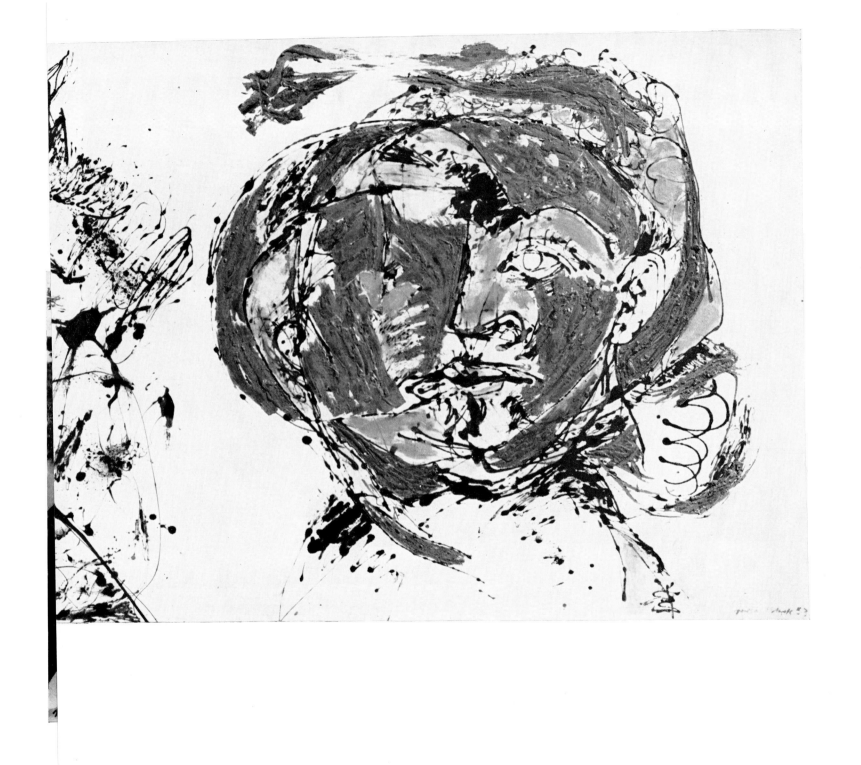

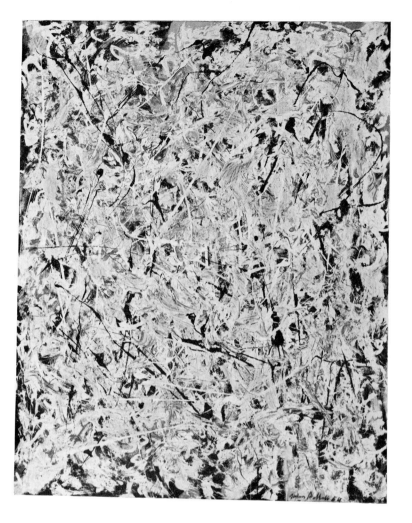

LEFT: *White Light.* 1954. Oil, enamel, and aluminum paint on canvas, $48\frac{3}{8}$ x $38\frac{1}{4}$ inches. Collection Mr. and Mrs. Sidney Janis, New York

OPPOSITE: *Scent.* 1955. Oil and enamel on canvas, 78 x $57\frac{1}{2}$ inches. Collection Mr. and Mrs. Frederick R. Weisman, Beverly Hills, California

The Deep. 1953. Oil and enamel on canvas, 86¾ x 59⅛ inches. Estate of the artist

Lenders to the Exhibition

Estate of the artist

Joachim Jean Aberbach, New York; Julian J. Aberbach, New York; Dr. and Mrs. David Abrahamsen, New York; Mr. and Mrs. Lester Avnet, New York; Mr. and Mrs. Walter Bareiss, Munich; Richard Brown Baker, New York; Thomas Hart Benton, Kansas City, Missouri; Mr. and Mrs. Crawford A. Black, New York; Dr. and Mrs. Bernard Brodsky, New York; Mr. and Mrs. Charles H. Carpenter, Jr., New Canaan, Connecticut; Edward F. Dragon, East Hampton, New York; Morton Feldman, New York; Herbert Ferber, New York; Mr. and Mrs. B. H. Friedman, New York; Mr. and Mrs. Roy J. Friedman, Chicago; David Gibbs, New York; Mr. and Mrs. Willard Gidwitz, Highland Park, Illinois; Charles Gimpel, London; Mr. and Mrs. I. Donald Grossman, New York; Mr. and Mrs. Stephen Hahn, New York; Mrs. Enid A. Haupt, New York; Joseph H. Hazen, New York; Mr. and Mrs. Ben Heller, New York; Dr. Joseph L. Henderson, San Francisco; Mrs. Kay Hillman, New York; Mrs. Cecil Blaffer Hudson, Houston; Sidney Janis, New York; Edwin Janss, Jr., Los Angeles; Mr. and Mrs. Frédéric E. Lake, New York; Mr. and Mrs. Alexander Liberman, New York; Miss Linda Lindeberg, New York; Mrs. H. Gates Lloyd, Haverford, Pennsylvania; Mr. and Mrs. Arnold Maremont, Winnetka, Illinois; Mr. and Mrs. Herbert Matter, New York; N. Richard Miller, Philadelphia; Mr. and Mrs. Hans Namuth, New York; Mr. and Mrs. Roy R. Neuberger, New York; Miss Katharine Ordway, Weston, Connecticut; Mrs. Paul Osborn, New York; Alfonso A. Ossorio, East Hampton, New York; Robert U. Ossorio, New York; Mrs. Bliss Parkinson, New York; Mrs. Betty Parsons, New York; Dr. and Mrs. Russel H. Patterson, Jr., New York; Miss Priscilla Peck, New York; Mr. and Mrs. G. H. Petersen, New York; Mrs. Penelope S. Potter, Amagansett, New York; Mrs. Ludwig B. Prosnitz, New York; Mr. and Mrs. Bernard J. Reis, New York; Dwight Ripley, Greenport, New York; Mrs. John D. Rockefeller 3rd, New York; Mr. and Mrs. Richard Rodgers, New York; Dr. and Mrs. Israel Rosen, Baltimore; William Rubin, New York; Mr. and Mrs. Stanley K. Sheinbaum, Santa Barbara, California; Mr. and Mrs. Joseph Slifka, New York; Mme Ileana Sonnabend, Paris; Mrs. Vicci Sperry, Los Angeles; M. and Mme Rodolphe Stadler, Paris; Mr. and Mrs. Harris B. Steinberg, New York; Mr. and Mrs. Davidson Taylor, New York; Mr. and Mrs. Burton Tremaine, Meriden, Connecticut; Mr. and Mrs. Theodore Wahl, Milford, New Jersey; Mrs. Emily Walker, West Redding, Connecticut; Dr. James H. Wall, White Plains, New York; Mr. and Mrs. Frederick R. Weisman, Beverly Hills, California; Mrs. Barnett Malbin (The Lydia and Harry Lewis Winston Collection), Birmingham, Michigan

Albright-Knox Art Gallery, Buffalo; The Art Institute of Chicago; Kunstsammlung Nordrhein-Westfalen, Düsseldorf; The Metropolitan Museum of Art, New York; The Museum of Modern Art, New York; Ohara Art Museum, Kurashiki City, Okayama Prefecture, Japan; San Francisco Museum of Art, San Francisco; School of Art, The University of Iowa, Iowa City; The Solomon R. Guggenheim Museum, New York; Staatsgalerie Stuttgart; Washington University, St. Louis; Whitney Museum of American Art, New York

Martha Jackson Gallery, New York; Sidney Janis Gallery, New York; Betty Parsons Gallery, New York

[131]

Catalogue of the Exhibition

Dimensions are given in feet and inches, height preceding width. Dimensions given for works on paper are sheet size. For prints, composition size is given for lithographs, plate size for engravings and etchings. Dates in parentheses do not appear on the works. In the case of "numbered" works that are also titled, the title precedes the number if the work was titled during the artist's lifetime; it follows the number if it became associated with the work after the artist's death. Mediums are defined as far as can be ascertained without scientific analysis.

WORKS ON CANVAS, COMPOSITION BOARD, WOOD, AND METAL

1. *Self-Portrait* (?). (1933?). Oil on gesso ground on canvas, mounted on composition board, $8\frac{1}{2}$ x $6\frac{1}{4}$ inches. Estate of the artist

2. *Woman.* (1934?). Oil on gesso ground on composition board, $14\frac{1}{8}$ x $10\frac{5}{8}$ inches. Estate of the artist. Ill. p. 19

3. *The Covered Wagon.* (1934). Oil on gesso ground on composition board, $10\frac{1}{8}$ x 13 inches. Estate of the artist. Ill. p. 82

4. *Going West.* (1934-35). Oil on gesso ground on composition board, $15\frac{1}{8}$ x $20\frac{7}{8}$ inches. Collection Thomas Hart Benton, Kansas City, Missouri. Ill. p. 82

5. *Landscape.* 1936. Oil on canvas, $23\frac{1}{2}$ x $29\frac{1}{2}$ inches. Collection Mrs. Ludwig B. Prosnitz, New York

6. *Menemsha Harbor.* 1936. Oil on canvas, $24\frac{1}{4}$ x $30\frac{1}{4}$ inches. Collection Dr. and Mrs. David Abrahamsen, New York

7. *Figures in a Landscape.* (1936?). Oil on canvas, $10\frac{3}{4}$ x $11\frac{7}{8}$ inches. Estate of the artist. Ill. p. 84

8. *The Flame.* (1937?). Oil on canvas, mounted on composition board, $20\frac{1}{8}$ x 30 inches. Estate of the artist. Ill. p. 84

9. *Untitled Composition.* (1937?). Oil on canvas, $15\frac{1}{8}$ x $20\frac{1}{8}$ inches. Estate of the artist

10. *Male and Female.* (1942). Oil on canvas, 73 x 49 inches. Collection Mrs. H. Gates Lloyd, Haverford, Pennsylvania. Ill. p. 87. (N. Y. only)

11. *The Guardians of the Secret.* 1943. Oil on canvas, $48\frac{3}{8}$ x $75\frac{1}{4}$ inches. San Francisco Museum of Art, Albert M. Bender Bequest Fund. Ill. p. 88

12. *The She-Wolf.* 1943. Oil on canvas, $41\frac{7}{8}$ x 67 inches. The Museum of Modern Art, New York. Ill. p. 86. (N. Y. only)

13. *Pasiphaë.* (1943). Oil on canvas, 4 feet 8 inches x 8 feet. Estate of the artist. Ill. p. 86

14. *Mural.* 1943. Oil on canvas, 7 feet $11\frac{3}{4}$ inches x 19 feet $9\frac{1}{2}$ inches. School of Art, The University of Iowa, Iowa City, gift of Peggy Guggenheim. Ill. pp. 90–91

15. *Gothic.* 1944. Oil and enamel on canvas, $84\frac{5}{8}$ x 56 inches. Estate of the artist. Ill. p. 90

16. *Night Ceremony.* (1944). Oil and enamel on canvas, 72 x $43\frac{1}{8}$ inches. Collection Mr. and Mrs. Bernard J. Reis, New York. Ill. p. 92

17. *The Night Dancer.* 1944. Oil on canvas, $43\frac{1}{4}$ x $33\frac{7}{8}$ inches. Collection Mr. and Mrs. Crawford A. Black, New York

18. *The Totem, Lesson I.* 1944. Oil on canvas, 70 x 44 inches. Collection Mrs. Emily Walker, West Redding, Connecticut

19. *Portrait of H. M.* (1945). Oil on canvas, $36\frac{1}{8}$ x $43\frac{1}{8}$ inches. School of Art, The University of Iowa, Iowa City, gift of Peggy Guggenheim. Ill. p. 89

20. *The Totem, Lesson II.* 1945. Oil on canvas, 72 x 60 inches. Estate of the artist. Ill. p. 93

21. *The Troubled Queen.* (1945). Oil and enamel on canvas, 74 x $43\frac{1}{2}$ inches. Collection Mr. and Mrs. Stephen Hahn, New York. Ill. p. 92

22. *Moon Vessel.* (1945). Oil and enamel on composition board, $33\frac{3}{8}$ x $17\frac{1}{2}$ inches. Lent by Mrs. Barnett Malbin (The Lydia and Harry Lewis Winston Collection), Birmingham, Michigan

23. *Blue (Moby Dick).* (1946). Gouache and ink on composition board, $18\frac{3}{4}$ x $23\frac{7}{8}$ inches. Ohara Art Museum, Kurashiki City, Okayama Prefecture, Japan. Ill. p. 94

24. *Red.* 1946. Gouache on composition board, $18\frac{3}{8}$ x $23\frac{1}{4}$ inches. Collection Mr. and Mrs. Charles H. Carpenter, Jr., New Canaan, Connecticut. Ill. p. 94

25. *Sounds in the Grass: Shimmering Substance.* (1946). Oil on canvas, $30\frac{1}{8}$ x $24\frac{1}{4}$ inches. Collection Mrs. Emily Walker, West Redding, Connecticut

26. *Sounds in the Grass: The Blue Unconscious.* 1946. Oil on canvas, 84 x 56 inches. Collection Mrs. Cecil Blaffer Hudson, Houston

27. *The White Angel.* (1946). Oil and enamel on canvas, $43\frac{1}{2}$ x $29\frac{5}{8}$ inches. Collection Mr. and Mrs. Stanley K. Sheinbaum, Santa Barbara, California

28. *Lucifer.* 1947. Oil, enamel, and aluminum paint on canvas, 41 inches x 8 feet $9\frac{1}{2}$ inches. Collection Joseph H. Hazen, New York. Ill. p. 99

29. *Vortex.* 1947. Oil and enamel on canvas, $20\frac{1}{4}$ x $18\frac{1}{4}$ inches. Collection Herbert Ferber, New York

30. *Full Fathom Five.* 1947. Oil on canvas with nails, tacks, buttons, keys, coins, cigarettes, matches, etc., $50\frac{7}{8}$ x $30\frac{1}{8}$ inches. The Museum of Modern Art, New York, gift of Peggy Guggenheim. Ill. p. 96

31. *Number 5, 1948.* Oil, enamel, and aluminum paint on composition board, 8 x 4 feet. Collection Alfonso A. Ossorio and Edward F. Dragon, East Hampton, New York. Ill. p. 97

32. *Summertime (Number 9, 1948).* Oil and enamel on canvas, $33\frac{1}{4}$ inches x 18 feet 2 inches. Estate of the artist. Ill. p. 98

33. *Arabesque (Number 13, 1948)*. Oil and enamel on canvas, 37¼ inches x 9 feet 8½ inches. Collection Richard Brown Baker, New York. Ill. p. 98

34. Untitled. 1948. Oil and enamel on metal, diameter 23⅛ inches. Collection Mr. and Mrs. Willard Gidwitz, Highland Park, Illinois. Ill. p. 101

35. *Number 4, 1949*. Oil, enamel, and aluminum paint with pebbles on canvas, mounted on composition board, 35⅝ x 34⅜ inches. Collection Miss Katharine Ordway, Weston, Connecticut

36. *Out of the Web (Number 7, 1949)*. Oil and enamel on composition board, cut out, 4 x 8 feet. Staatsgalerie Stuttgart. Ill. p. 104

37. *Number 8, 1949*. Oil, enamel, and aluminum paint on canvas, 34⅛ x 71¼ inches. Collection Mr. and Mrs. Roy R. Neuberger, New York. Ill. p. 105

38. *Number 10, 1949*. Enamel and aluminum paint on canvas, mounted on wood, 18 inches x 8 feet 11¼ inches. Collection Alfonso A. Ossorio, East Hampton, New York

39. *Number 23, 1949*. Oil and enamel on canvas, mounted on composition board, 26½ x 12⅛ inches. Collection Mrs. John D. Rockefeller 3rd, New York

40. *Number 24, Number 25, Number 29 (Triptych)*. 1949. Enamel on canvas, mounted on composition board; left panel 26¾ x 12 inches, center panel 27⅞ x 11⅜ inches, right panel 17¼ x 14⅞ inches. Collection Mr. and Mrs. Stanley K. Sheinbaum, Santa Barbara, California

41. *Number 26, 1949*. Oil and enamel on canvas, 23⅛ x 14 inches. Sidney Janis Gallery, New York

42. *White on Black*. 1949. Oil on canvas, 24⅛ x 17¼ inches. Sidney Janis Gallery, New York. Ill. p. 103

43. Untitled. (1949). Oil and enamel on canvas, mounted on composition board, 10 inches x 10 feet 1⅞ inches. Collection Mr. and Mrs. Joseph Slifka, New York

44. Untitled. (1950). Oil, enamel, and aluminum paint on canvas, mounted on composition board, 12⅛ x 13 inches. Collection Mr. and Mrs. Frédéric E. Lake, New York

45. *Lavender Mist (Number 1, 1950)*. Oil, enamel, and aluminum paint on canvas, 7 feet 3 inches x 9 feet 10 inches. Collection Alfonso A. Ossorio and Edward F. Dragon, East Hampton, New York. Ill. p. 107. (N. Y. only)

46. *Number 7, 1950*. Oil, enamel, and aluminum paint on canvas, 24¼ inches x 9 feet 1¾ inches. Collection Mr. and Mrs. Joseph Slifka, New York

47. *Number 8, 1950*. Oil, enamel, and aluminum paint on canvas, mounted on composition board, 56⅛ x 39 inches. Collection Mrs. Enid A. Haupt, New York. Ill. p. 113. (N. Y. only)

48. *Number 17, 1950 (Fireworks)*. Enamel and aluminum paint on composition board, 22¼ x 22¼ inches. Collection Robert U. Ossorio, New York

49. *Number 27, 1950*. Oil, enamel, and aluminum paint on canvas, 4 feet 1 inch x 8 feet 10 inches. Whitney Museum of American Art, New York. Ill. p. 105

50. *Autumn Rhythm (Number 30, 1950)*. Oil and enamel on canvas, 8 feet 10½ inches x 17 feet 8 inches. The Metropolitan Museum of Art, New York, George A. Hearn Fund, 1957. Ill. pp. 108–9. (N. Y. only)

51. *One (Number 31, 1950)*. Oil and enamel on canvas, 8 feet 10 inches x 17 feet 5 inches. Collection Mr. and Mrs. Ben Heller, New York. Ill. p. 106

52. *Number 32, 1950*. Enamel on canvas, 8 feet 10 inches x 15 feet. Kunstsammlung Nordrhein-Westfalen, Düsseldorf. Ill. pp. 8–9. (N.Y. only)

53. Untitled. 1950. Oil, enamel, and aluminum paint on canvas, 36⅝ x 25⅝ inches. Collection N. Richard Miller, Philadelpha. Ill. p. 110

54. Untitled. (1950). Enamel on canvas, 24 x 79⅞ inches. Collection Mr. and Mrs. I. Donald Grossman, New York

55. *Mural*. 1950. Oil, enamel, and aluminum paint on canvas, mounted on wood, 6 x 8 feet. Collection William Rubin, New York. Ill. p. 111

56. Untitled. (1950). Oil and enamel on canvas, mounted on composition board, 17¼ x 9¼ inches. Collection Mr. and Mrs. Richard Rodgers, New York

57. *Number 3, 1951 (Image of Man)*. Enamel on canvas, 56 x 24 inches. Collection Robert U. Ossorio, New York. Ill. p. 115

58. *Number 9, 1951*. Enamel on canvas, 57⅛ x 38⅜ inches. Estate of the artist

59. *Number 10, 1951*. Enamel on canvas, mounted on composition board, 59⅞ x 29 inches. Collection Alfonso A. Ossorio and Edward F. Dragon, East Hampton, New York. Ill. p. 117

60. *Number 11, 1951*. Enamel on canvas, 4 feet 9½ inches x 11 feet 6 inches. Estate of the artist. Ill. p. 118

60a. *Number 14, 1951*. Oil on canvas, 4 feet 9⅝ inches x 8 feet 10 inches. Estate of the artist. Ill. p. 119. (Added during the exhibition)

61. *Number 18, 1951*. Enamel on canvas, 58¾ x 55½ inches. Collection Alfonso A. Ossorio and Edward F. Dragon, East Hampton, New York

62. *Number 23, 1951 (Frogman)*. Enamel on canvas, 58⅝ x 47¼ inches. Martha Jackson Gallery, New York. Ill. p. 115

63. *Echo (Number 25, 1951)*. Enamel on canvas, 7 feet 8 inches x 7 feet 1¾ inches. Collection Mr. and Mrs. Ben Heller, New York. Ill. p. 114

64. *Number 27, 1951*. Enamel on canvas, 55⅝ x 75⅛ inches. Estate of the artist

65. *Number 28, 1951.* Oil on canvas, 30⅛ x 54⅛ inches. Collection Mr. and Mrs. Arnold Maremont, Winnetka, Illinois. (N.Y. only)

66. Untitled. 1951. Oil, enamel, and aluminum paint on canvas, 27 x 25 inches. Sidney Janis Gallery, New York

67. *Black and White Painting.* (1951–52). Enamel on canvas, 34½ x 30⅝ inches. Collection Dr. and Mrs. Russel H. Patterson, Jr., New York

68. *Number 3, 1952.* Enamel on canvas, 55⅞ x 66 inches. Collection Alfonso A. Ossorio and Edward F. Dragon, East Hampton, New York. Ill. p. 122

69. *Number 6, 1952.* Enamel on canvas, 56⅛ x 47⅛ inches. Collection Mme Ileana Sonnabend, Paris

70. *Number 7, 1952.* Enamel on canvas, 53⅛ x 40 inches. Estate of the artist. Ill. p. 116

71. *Convergence (Number 10, 1952).* Enamel on canvas, 7 feet 9½ inches x 13 feet. Albright-Knox Art Gallery, Buffalo, New York, gift of Seymour H. Knox. Ill. p. 121

72. *Blue Poles (Number 11, 1952).* (Subsequently inscribed 1953). Enamel and aluminum paint with glass on canvas, 6 feet 11 inches x 16 feet. Collection Mr. and Mrs. Ben Heller, New York. Ill. p. 120

73. *Portrait and a Dream.* 1953. Enamel on canvas, 4 feet 10¼ inches x 11 feet 2½ inches. Acquired for the Dallas Museum of Fine Arts by Mr. and Mrs. Algur Hurtle Meadows. Ill. pp. 124–25

74. *Easter and the Totem.* 1953. Oil on canvas, 82¼ x 58 inches. Estate of the artist. Ill. p. 123

75. *The Deep.* 1953. Oil and enamel on canvas, 86¾ x 59⅛ inches. Estate of the artist. Ill. p. 130

76. *Four Opposites.* 1953. Oil, enamel, and aluminum paint on canvas, 72½ x 51⅜ inches. Collection Edwin Janss, Jr., Los Angeles

77. *Ocean Greyness.* 1953. Oil and enamel on canvas, 57¾ x 90 inches. The Solomon R. Guggenheim Museum, New York. Ill. p. 126

78. *Sleeping Effort.* 1953. Oil and enamel on canvas, 49¾ x 76⅛ inches. Washington University, St. Louis, Missouri. Ill. p. 127

79. *Frieze.* 1953–55. Oil, enamel, and aluminum paint on canvas, 26 inches x 7 feet. Collection Mr. and Mrs. Burton Tremaine, Meriden, Connecticut. (N. Y. only)

80. *White Light.* 1954. Oil, enamel, and aluminum paint on canvas, 48⅜ x 38¼ inches. Collection Mr. and Mrs. Sidney Janis, New York. Ill. p. 128

81. *Search* 1955. Oil and enamel on canvas, 57⅞ x 90¼ inches. Collection Mrs. Vicci Sperry, Los Angeles

82. *Scent.* 1955. Oil and enamel on canvas, 78 x 57½ inches. Collection Mr. and Mrs. Frederick R. Weisman, Beverly Hills, California. Ill. p. 129

WORKS ON PAPER, AND WORKS ON PAPER MOUNTED ON CANVAS AND COMPOSITION BOARD

Mediums given for early works on paper include the instrument used in contact with the surface (e.g., brush or pen); in later works, in which the primary method of application is drip, no instrument is cited.

83. Page from a Sketchbook. (1937–38). Brush, pen and ink, 12 x 8⅞ inches. Estate of the artist

Four pages from a sketchbook (1938):

84. Studies after Michelangelo's *Jonah* and *Nude Youth,* from the Sistine Chapel Ceiling. Colored pencil, 17⅞ x 11⅞ inches. Estate of the artist

85. Studies after El Greco's *Healing of the Blind Man* and *Cleansing of the Temple.* Colored pencil, pencil, 17⅞ x 11⅞ inches. Estate of the artist. Ill. p. 83

86. Self-Portrait with Studies after El Greco's *Healing of the Blind Man, Holy Family,* and *Betrothal of the Virgin.* Colored pencil, pencil, 17⅞ x 11⅞ inches. Estate of the artist. Ill. p. 83

87. Life Studies. Colored pencil, pencil, 17⅞ x 11⅞ inches. Estate of the artist

Six pages from a sketchbook (1938):

88. Study after Michelangelo's *The Great Flood,* from the Sistine Chapel Ceiling. Colored pencil, pencil, pen and ink, wash, 13¾ x 16⅞ inches. Estate of the artist

89. Studies after El Greco's *Annunciation, Madonna on Throne of Clouds with Saints Agnes and Marina,* and *Saint Joseph with the Child Jesus.* Colored pencil, pencil, brush and ink, 16⅞ x 13¾ inches. Estate of the artist

90. Studies after El Greco's *Coronation of the Virgin.* Colored pencil, pencil, 16⅞ x 13¾ inches. Estate of the artist

91. Studies after Rubens' *Peace and War* and *Diana and Endymion.* Colored pencil, pencil, 16⅞ x 13¾ inches. Estate of the artist

92. Study after Michelangelo's *Nude Youth,* from the Sistine Chapel Ceiling. Colored pencil, pencil, 16⅞ x 13¾ inches. Estate of the artist

93. Composition with figures after Michelangelo's *The Last Judgment,* from the Sistine Chapel. Colored pencil, pencil, 16⅞ x 13¾ inches. Estate of the artist

94. *Figure in a Landscape.* (1938). Crayon, pencil, 11¼ x 14⅜ inches. Estate of the artist. Ill. p. 83

95. *Deep-Sea Diver's Helmet.* (1938–39). Crayon, colored pencil, pencil, 8⅜ x 5⅜ inches. Estate of the artist

96. *A Pair of Figures Entwined.* (1938–39). Crayon, pencil, 14 x 11 inches. Estate of the artist

97. Studies with a Bull, Horse, and Screaming Heads. (1939–40). Colored pencil, pencil,

crayon, pen and ink on gray cardboard, $13\frac{7}{8}$ x $10\frac{7}{8}$ inches. Estate of the artist

98. *Head.* (1939–40). Pencil, pastel on brown paper, 6 x $8\frac{3}{8}$ inches. Collection Dr. Joseph L. Henderson, San Francisco

99. *Head.* (1939–40). Pencil, pastel on blue paper, 6 x 8 inches. Collection Dr. Joseph L. Henderson, San Francisco

100. *Horse and Figure.* (1939–40). Crayon, 15 x 11 inches. Collection Dr. Joseph L. Henderson, San Francisco

101. Studies. (1939–40). Colored pencil, pencil, crayon, brush and colored ink, pen and black ink, 14 x 11 inches. Collection Dr. Joseph L. Henderson, San Francisco. Ill. p. 85

102. Studies. (1939–40). Colored pencil, crayon, pen and ink, 14 x 11 inches. Collection Dr. Joseph L. Henderson, San Francisco. Ill. p. 85

103. *Landscape.* (1940–41). Crayon, brush, pen and ink, $8\frac{7}{8}$ x 12 inches (irregular). Estate of the artist

104. Study. (1940–41). Crayon, brush, pen and ink, 12 x $8\frac{7}{8}$ inches. Estate of the artist

105. Page from a Sketchbook. (1941, subsequently inscribed 1938). Brush and ink, crayon, $17\frac{5}{8}$ x $13\frac{7}{8}$ inches. Estate of the artist

106. Figure Composition. (1941). Gouache, pencil, $21\frac{7}{8}$ x $30\frac{1}{4}$ inches (sight). Collection Joan and Lester Avnet, New York

107. Study. (1941). Watercolor, pastel, pencil, brush, pen and ink, 13 x $10\frac{1}{4}$ inches. Collection Joan and Lester Avnet, New York. Ill. p. 85

108. Sheet of Studies with Heads. (1941). Watercolor, pencil, crayon, pen and ink, $17\frac{7}{8}$ x $13\frac{7}{8}$ inches. Collection Joan and Lester Avnet, New York. Ill. p. 85

109. Sheet of Studies with a Bull. (1941). Pen and ink, $17\frac{7}{8}$ x $13\frac{7}{8}$ inches. Estate of the artist. Ill. p. 85

110. *Animals and Figures.* 1942. Oil, gouache, pen and ink, $22\frac{3}{8}$ x $29\frac{7}{8}$ inches. The Museum of Modern Art, New York, Mr. and Mrs. Donald B. Straus Fund

111. Untitled. (1942–43). Oil, brush, spatter, pen and ink, $20\frac{1}{8}$ x $13\frac{1}{4}$ inches. Collection Charles Gimpel, London

112. *Animal and Figure.* (1943). Pen and ink on blue paper, $11\frac{1}{2}$ x $6\frac{3}{8}$ inches. Estate of the artist

113. Studies with a Bull and Figures. (1943). Pen and ink, $19\frac{3}{4}$ x $12\frac{3}{4}$ inches. Estate of the artist

114. *Horse and Woman.* (1943). Pen and ink, 10 x $12\frac{7}{8}$ inches. Estate of the artist

115. Untitled. (1943). Crayon, pen and ink, $22\frac{1}{8}$ x $27\frac{1}{4}$ inches. Collection Mr. and Mrs. Harris B. Steinberg, New York

116. Untitled. (1943). Brush, pen and ink, colored pencil brushed with water, $18\frac{3}{4}$ x $24\frac{3}{4}$ inches. Estate of the artist. Ill. p. 89

117. Untitled. (1943). Brush, pen and ink, colored pencil brushed with water, $18\frac{3}{4}$ x $24\frac{3}{4}$ inches. Inscribed: *the effort of the dance/the city with horns/the thickness of white.* Collection Mr. and Mrs. Bernard J. Reis, New York. Ill. p. 89

118. Untitled. (1943). Collage of colored papers with brush, pen and ink, crayon, colored pencil brushed with water, $15\frac{1}{2}$ x $13\frac{5}{8}$ inches. Collection Mr. and Mrs. Frederick R. Weisman, Beverly Hills, California. Ill. p. 87

119. Untitled. 1943. Gouache, 23 x $29\frac{1}{8}$ inches. Collection Mr. and Mrs. Davidson Taylor, New York. Ill. p. 88. (N. Y. only)

120. Untitled. 1942–44. Brush and ink, colored pencil, crayon, sgraffito, $12\frac{5}{8}$ x $10\frac{1}{8}$ inches (irregular). Inscribed: *For H.F.* Betty Parsons Gallery, New York

121. Untitled. (1944?). Brush, pen and black and colored inks, gouache, pastel, wash, sgraffito, $18\frac{3}{4}$ x $24\frac{3}{4}$ inches. Collection Mr. and Mrs. Alexander Liberman, New York. Ill. p. 95

122. Untitled. 1944. Brush, spatter, pen and black and colored inks, $18\frac{3}{4}$ x $24\frac{3}{4}$ inches. The Art Institute of Chicago. Ill. p. 95

123. Untitled. 1944. Brush, spatter, pen and black and colored inks, sgraffito, $18\frac{3}{8}$ x $24\frac{3}{8}$ inches. Collection James H. Wall, White Plains, New York

124. Untitled. 1944. Gouache, brush, pen and ink, wash, $22\frac{1}{2}$ x $30\frac{5}{8}$ inches. Inscribed: *To Paul Osborn.* Collection Mrs. Paul Osborn, New York

125. Untitled. 1944. Brush and ink, colored pencil, sgraffito, $8\frac{1}{4}$ x $7\frac{1}{4}$ inches. Collection Dr. and Mrs. Israel Rosen, Baltimore

126. Untitled. (1945). Gouache, pastel, brush, spatter, pen and black and colored inks, sgraffito, $22\frac{1}{2}$ x $15\frac{1}{4}$ inches (irregular). Collection Mrs. Kay Hillman, New York

127. Untitled. 1945. Enamel, pastel, $25\frac{3}{4}$ x $20\frac{1}{2}$ inches. Collection Mr. and Mrs. Walter Bareiss, Munich

128. Untitled. (1945). Oil, gouache, pastel, pen and ink, $30\frac{5}{8}$ x $22\frac{3}{8}$ inches. The Museum of Modern Art, New York, Blanchette Rockefeller Fund

129. Untitled. (1946). Crayon, pastel, brush, drip, pen and ink on brown paper, $18\frac{7}{8}$ x $24\frac{5}{8}$ inches. Collection Dr. and Mrs. Bernard Brodsky, New York

130. Untitled. 1946. Spatter, pen and black and colored inks, gouache, wash, sgraffito, $22\frac{3}{8}$ x $30\frac{3}{8}$ inches. Collection Dwight Ripley, Greenport, New York

131. Untitled. (1946). Pen and black and colored inks, pastel, gouache, wash, $22\frac{1}{2}$ x $30\frac{7}{8}$ inches. Collection Dwight Ripley, Greenport, New York. Ill. p. 95

132. Untitled. (1946). Brush, pen and black and colored inks, pastel, gouache, wash, $22\frac{1}{2}$ x $30\frac{5}{8}$ inches. Collection Dwight Ripley, Greenport, New York. Ill. p. 95

133. Untitled. (1946). Pen and ink, $4\frac{7}{8}$ x $11\frac{3}{8}$ inches. Collection Mrs. Betty Parsons, New York

134. Untitled. 1947. Pen and ink, crayon, $17\frac{3}{4}$ x $23\frac{1}{4}$ inches (sight). Inscribed: *For Betty 1951 Jan 30 J P*. Collection Mrs. Betty Parsons, New York

135. Untitled. 1947. Crayon, colored pencil, brush, pen and ink, $20\frac{1}{2}$ x $25\frac{7}{8}$ inches. Estate of the artist

136. *War*. 1947. Brush, pen and ink, crayon, $20\frac{1}{2}$ x 26 inches. Estate of the artist

137. Untitled. (1947). Brush, spatter, pen and black and colored inks, $18\frac{3}{4}$ x $24\frac{7}{8}$ inches. Collection Julian J. and Joachim Jean Aberbach, New York

138. Untitled. 1948. Collage of paper with oil, enamel on wet gesso, $22\frac{1}{8}$ x $30\frac{5}{8}$ inches. Collection Mr. and Mrs. G. H. Petersen, New York. Ill. p. 101. (N. Y. only)

139. *Number 12, 1948 (Yellow, Gray, Black)*. Enamel on wet gesso, $22\frac{1}{2}$ x $30\frac{5}{8}$ inches. Collection Mrs. Betty Parsons, New York. Ill. p. 101

140. *Number 14, 1948 (Gray)*. Enamel on wet gesso, $22\frac{3}{4}$ x 31 inches. Collection Miss Katharine Ordway, Weston, Connecticut. Ill. p. 101

141. *Number 12, 1949*. Enamel on paper, mounted on composition board, 31 x $22\frac{1}{2}$ inches. The Museum of Modern Art, New York, gift of Edgar Kaufmann, Jr. Ill. p. 102

142. *Number 15, 1949*. Enamel, aluminum paint on gesso ground on paper, mounted on composition board, 31 x $22\frac{3}{8}$ inches. Collection Miss Priscilla Peck, New York. Ill. p. 102

143. *Number 19, 1949*. Enamel on parchment, mounted on composition board, 31 x $22\frac{5}{8}$ inches. Collection Dr. and Mrs. Israel Rosen, Baltimore. Ill. p. 102

144. *Birds of Paradise (Number 30, 1949)*. Enamel, aluminum paint on paper, mounted on composition board, $30\frac{3}{4}$ x $22\frac{1}{2}$ inches. Collection Dr. and Mrs. David Abrahamsen, New York. Ill. p. 103

145. *Number 31, 1949*. Oil, enamel, aluminum paint on gesso ground on paper, mounted on composition board, $30\frac{1}{4}$ x $22\frac{1}{8}$ inches. Collection Mr. and Mrs. Roy J. Friedman, Chicago. (N. Y. only)

146. *Number 33, 1949*. Enamel, aluminum paint on gesso ground on paper, mounted on composition board, $22\frac{1}{2}$ x 31 inches. Collection Robert U. Ossorio, New York

147. *Green Silver*. (1949). Enamel, aluminum paint on paper, mounted on canvas, $22\frac{7}{8}$ x $30\frac{7}{8}$ inches. Collection Mr. and Mrs. Joseph Slifka, New York. Ill. p. 103

148. Untitled. (1949). Collage of cloth, paper, cut composition board with enamel, aluminum paint, $30\frac{7}{8}$ x $22\frac{1}{2}$ inches. Collection Julian J. and Joachim Jean Aberbach, New York

149. Untitled. (1950?). Enamel, 31 x 23 inches. Collection Mr. and Mrs. Herbert Matter, New York

150. Untitled. (1950). Ink, $13\frac{7}{8}$ x $22\frac{1}{4}$ inches (sight). Collection Mrs. Bliss Parkinson, New York

151. Untitled. (1950?). Ink on rice paper, $28\frac{7}{8}$ x 21 inches. Estate of the artist

152. Untitled. 1951. Ink on Japan paper, $17\frac{1}{2}$ x $22\frac{1}{4}$ inches. Collection Morton Feldman, New York

153. Untitled. (1951). Ink on rice paper, $24\frac{3}{8}$ x $34\frac{1}{2}$ inches. Collection David Gibbs, New York

154. Untitled. 1951. Sepia ink on rice paper, $24\frac{7}{8}$ x $39\frac{1}{8}$ inches. Collection Mrs. Penelope S. Potter, Amagansett, New York

155. *Number 3, 1951*. Ink on rice paper, 25 x $38\frac{7}{8}$ inches. Collection Mr. and Mrs. Alexander Liberman, New York

156. Untitled. 1951. Sepia and black ink on rice paper, $24\frac{7}{8}$ x 39 inches (irregular). Collection N. Richard Miller, Philadelphia

157. *Number 17, 1951*. Watercolor, black and colored inks on Howell paper, $17\frac{5}{8}$ x $22\frac{1}{8}$ inches (irregular). Collection Robert U. Ossorio, New York

158. *Number 18, 1951*. Watercolor, ink on rice paper, $24\frac{7}{8}$ x $38\frac{3}{4}$ inches. Collection Linda Lindeberg, New York

159. Untitled. (1951). Watercolor, ink on rice paper, $24\frac{1}{4}$ x 34 inches. Estate of the artist. Ill. p. 112

160. Untitled. 1951. Watercolor, ink on rice paper, $24\frac{1}{2}$ x 34 inches. Collection Mr. and Mrs. B. H. Friedman, New York. Ill. p. 112

161. Untitled. 1951. Ink, wash on Howell paper, mounted on canvas, $17\frac{5}{8}$ x $21\frac{5}{8}$ inches. Collection Rodolphe and Mic Stadler, Paris

162. Untitled. 1951. Watercolor, black and colored inks on Howell paper, 13 x $16\frac{1}{4}$ inches. Collection Mr. and Mrs. Hans Namuth, New York

163. Untitled. 1951. Watercolor, ink, gesso, cloth on Howell paper, mounted on canvas, 20 x $25\frac{1}{2}$ inches. Inscribed: *For Lyn F.* Lent anonymously

164. Untitled. (1953–54). Brush and black and colored inks on Howell paper, $15\frac{3}{4}$ x $20\frac{1}{2}$ inches. The Museum of Modern Art, New York, gift of Mr. and Mrs. Ira Haupt. Ill. p. 122

165. Untitled. (1956). Watercolor, ink on Howell paper, $17\frac{3}{4}$ x $22\frac{1}{8}$ inches. Estate of the artist

166. Untitled. (1956). Black and colored inks, cloth on Howell paper, $17\frac{3}{8}$ x $21\frac{1}{4}$ inches (irregular). Estate of the artist

PRINTS

167. *Lone Rider*. (1934–35). Lithograph, $5\frac{3}{4}$ x 8 inches (irregular). Collection Theodore Wahl, Milford, New Jersey

168. *Plowing.* (1936). Lithograph, $7\frac{1}{2}$ x $11\frac{1}{4}$ inches (irregular). Collection Theodore Wahl, Milford, New Jersey

169. *Farm Workers.* (1936–37). Lithograph, $7\frac{3}{8}$ x $11\frac{3}{8}$ inches (irregular). Collection Theodore Wahl, Milford, New Jersey

170. *Coal Miners.* (1938). Lithograph, $11\frac{1}{4}$ x 15 inches (irregular). Collection Theodore Wahl, Milford, New Jersey

171. *Figures in a Landscape.* (1938). Lithograph, 10 x $14\frac{1}{2}$ inches (irregular). Collection Theodore Wahl, Milford, New Jersey

172. *Untitled.* (1944). Engraving and drypoint, $14\frac{7}{8}$ x $17\frac{5}{8}$ inches. Estate of the artist

Bibliography

POLLOCK STATEMENTS, WRITINGS, INTERVIEWS, AND LETTERS
(arranged chronologically)

1. [Answers to a questionnaire.] *Arts & Architecture,* LXI, February 1944, p. 14.

2. [Statement.] *in* JANIS, SIDNEY. *Abstract & Surrealist Art in America.* New York: Reynal & Hitchcock, 1944. P. 112.

3. "My Painting," *Possibilities* (New York), Winter 1947/48, pp. 78ff.

4. [Excerpts from an interview taped by William Wright, Springs, Long Island, 1950.] *Art in America* (New York), LIII, August–September 1965, pp. 111f.

5. "Unframed Space," *New Yorker,* XXVI, August 5, 1950, p. 16.
   Interview with Jackson and Lee Pollock.

6. [Narration for the film *Jackson Pollock* made by Hans Namuth and Paul Falkenberg, 1951.] Typescript in the Library, The Museum of Modern Art, New York.

7. [Excerpt from a letter to Alfonso Ossorio and Edward Dragon, June 7, 1951.] *in* LOS ANGELES COUNTY MUSEUM OF ART. *New York School. The First Generation. Paintings of the 1940s and 1950s.* 1965.
   See No. 215.

8. [Statements.] *in* RODMAN, SELDEN. *Conversations with Artists.* New York: Devin-Adair, 1957. Pp. 76–87.

MONOGRAPHS

9. O'CONNOR, FRANCIS V. "The Genesis of Jackson Pollock: 1912 to 1943." Unpublished Ph.D. dissertation, The Johns Hopkins University, Baltimore, 1965.

10. O'HARA, FRANK. *Jackson Pollock.* (The Great American Artists Series.) New York: George Braziller, 1959.
    rev.: Folds, Thomas M., in *College Art Journal* (New York), XX, Fall 1960, pp. 52f.

11. ROBERTSON, BRYAN. *Jackson Pollock.* New York: Harry N. Abrams, Inc., 1960.
    British ed.: London, Thames & Hudson, 1960 – German ed.: Cologne, DuMont Schauberg, 1961.
    rev.: Archer, W. G., in *Studio* (London), CLXI, April 1961, p. 161; Frampton, Kenneth, in *Arts Review* (London), XIII, June 3–17, 1961, p. 2; Rosenberg, Harold, in *Art News* (New York), LIX, February 1961, pp. 35ff; Tyler, Parker, Letter to the editor in response to Rosenberg review, *Art News,* LX, March 1961, p. 6; *Times Literary Supplement* (London), February 3, 1961, p. 70.

GENERAL WORKS

12. ASHTON, DORE. *The Unknown Shore: A View of Contemporary Art.* Boston and Toronto: Little, Brown & Company, 1962.

    BAUR, JOHN I. H., *see* No. 16.

13. BLESH, RUDI. *Modern Art USA, Men, Rebellion, Conquest, 1900–1956.* New York: Alfred A. Knopf, 1956.

14. CANDEE, MARJORIE DENT (ed.). "Pollock, Jackson," *Current Biography Yearbook.* New York: H. W. Wilson, 1956.

15. C[HOAY], F[RANÇOISE]. "Pollock," *Dictionary of Modern Painting,* eds. Carlton Lake and Robert Maillard. 3rd ed. New York: Tudor, 1964.
    Tr. from the French *Dictionnaire de la peinture moderne.* Paris: Hazan, 1955.

16. GOODRICH, LLOYD and BAUR, JOHN I. H. *American Art of Our Century.* New York: Frederick A. Praeger, 1961.

17. GUGGENHEIM, PEGGY. *Confessions of an Art Addict.* New York: Macmillan, 1960.
    rev. ed. of *Out of This Century.* New York: Dial, 1946.

18. HAFTMANN, WERNER. *Painting in the Twentieth Century.* 2 vols. New York: Frederick A. Praeger, 1960; new and expanded ed., 1965. German eds.: Munich, Prestel Verlag, 1954–55; rev. ed., 1957.

19. HESS, THOMAS B. *Abstract Painting.* New York: Viking, 1951.

20. HUNTER, SAM. "Jackson Pollock: The Maze and the Minotaur," *New World Writing.* (Ninth Mentor Selection.) New York: New American Library, 1956.

21. ———. *Modern American Painting and Sculpture.* New York: Dell, 1959.

22. ———. "USA," *Art Since 1945.* New York: Harry N. Abrams, Inc., 1958.

23. LINDE, ULF. *Spejare*. Stockholm: Bonnier, 1960.
  In Swedish.

24. PIERRE, JOSE. "Surrealism, Jackson Pollock and Lyric-Abstraction," *in* NEW YORK. D'ARCY GALLERIES. *Surrealist Intrusion in the Enchanters' Domain*. 1960.

25. PONENTE, NELLO. *Modern Painting. Contemporary Trends*. Lausanne: Albert Skira, 1960.

26. SEUPHOR, MICHEL. *Dictionary of Abstract Painting*. New York: Paris Book Center, 1957.
  Tr. from the French *Dictionnaire de la peinture abstraite*. Paris: Hazan, 1957.

27. SOBY, JAMES THRALL. *Contemporary Painters*. New York: The Museum of Modern Art, 1948.

28. ———. "Jackson Pollock," *New Art in America*, ed. John I. H. Baur. Greenwich, Conn.: New York Graphic Society and New York: Frederick Praeger, 1957.

ARTICLES AND MISCELLANEOUS REFERENCES

29. ALFIERI, BRUNO. "Piccolo discorso sui quadri di Jackson Pollock," *L'Arte Moderna* [date and place of publication not known].

30. ALLOWAY, LAWRENCE. "U.S. Modern: Paintings," *Art News and Review* (London), VII, January 21, 1956, pp. 1, 9.

31. ———. "Background to Action. 2. The Marks," *Art News and Review* (London), IX, October 26, 1957, pp. 1–2.

32. ———. "The Art of Jackson Pollock: 1912–1956," *Listener* (London), LX, November 27, 1958, p. 888.

33. ———. "London Chronicle," *Art International*, II, December 1958–January 1959, pp. 33–34, 73.

34. ———. "Sign and Surface. Notes on Black and White Painting in New York," *Quadrum* 9, 1960, pp. 49–62.

35. ———. "Notes on Pollock," *Art International*, V, May 1961, pp. 38–41.
  ———, *see* Nos. 207–210.

36. "Americans Abroad," *Time*, LVI, August 21, 1950, p. 49.
  ARCHER, W. G., *see* No. 11.

37. ARMSTRONG, RICHARD. "Abstract Expressionism Was an American Revolution," *Canadian Art*, XXI, September/October 1964, pp. 263–65.

38. "Art of Jackson Pollock," *Times* (London), November 7, 1958.

39. ASHTON, DORE. [Reviews.] *Arts & Architecture*, LXXIII, January 1956, pp. 10ff; LXXIV, March 1957, pp. 10f; LXXVI, January 1959, p. 6.

40. ———. "Perspective de la peinture américaine," *Cahiers d'Art*, XXXIII–XXXV, 1960, pp. 203–20.

41. ———. "Pollock: Le nouvel espace," *XXe Siècle*, XXIII, December 1961, pp. 75–80.

42. BARR, ALFRED H., JR. "Gorky, de Kooning, Pollock," *Art News*, XLIX, Summer 1950, pp. 22–23.

43. BAYL, FRIEDRICH. "Jackson Pollock," *Die Kunst und das schöne Heim* (Munich), LIX, June 1961, pp. 330–33.

44. BERGER, JOHN. "The White Cell," *New Statesman*, LVI, November 22, 1958, pp. 722–23.

45. "The Best?" *Time*, L, December 1, 1947, p. 55.

46. BRECHT, HERBERT. "Chance-Imagery," *Collage* (Palermo), Nos. 3–4, December 1964, pp. 71–79.

47. BURROWS, CARLYLE. [Review.] *Herald Tribune*, November 27, 1949.

48. C., M. [Review.] *Burlington Magazine*, C, December 1958, p. 450.

49. CALVESI, MAURIZIO. "Genio di Pollock," *I 4 Soli*, V, March–April 1958, pp. 19–21.

50. "The Champ," *Time*, LXVI, December 19, 1955, pp. 64, 66.

50a. "Chaos, Damn It," *Time*, LVI, November 20, 1950, pp. 70–71.
  Response by Pollock in Letters to the Editor, December 11, 1950, p. 10.

51. CHOAY, FRANÇOISE. "Jackson Pollock," *L'Oeil*, No. 43/44, July–August 1958, pp. 42ff.

52. CLARK, ELIOT. "New York Commentary," *Studio* (London), CLIII, June 1957, pp. 184–85.

53. COATES, ROBERT M. [Reviews.] *New Yorker*, May 29, 1943, p. 49; November 20, 1943, p. 97; January 17, 1948, p. 57; December 3, 1949, p. 95; December 9, 1950, pp. 109–11; November 22, 1952, pp. 178–79; February 20, 1954, pp. 81–82; December 29, 1956, pp. 47–49; November 16, 1957, p. 222.

54. CONNOLLY, JEAN. [Reviews.] *Nation*, May 1, 1943, p. 643; May 29, 1943, p. 786.

54a. COOPER, DOUGLAS. "The Biennale Exhibition in Venice," *Listener* (London), XLIV, July 6, 1950, pp. 12–14.

55. CREHAN, HUBERT. "Pollock: A Janus-Headed Show," *Art Digest*, XXVIII, February 15, 1954, pp. 15f.

56. CRISPOLTI, ENRICO. "Appunti su Jackson Pollock," *I 4 Soli*, IV, January–February 1957, pp. 8–10.

57. C[URJEL], H[ANS]. "Jackson Pollock," *Werk*, XLVIII, December 1961, pp. 274–76.

58. DEVREE, HOWARD. [Reviews.] *New York Times*, March 25, 1945; December 3, 1950; December 2, 1951; November 16, 1952.

59. D[REXLER], A[RTHUR]. "Unframed Space: A Museum for Jackson Pollock's Paintings," *Interiors*, CIX, January 1950, p. 90.

60. FAISON, S. LANE, JR. [Reviews.] *Nation*, December 13, 1952, p. 564; February 20, 1954, pp. 154, 156.

61. FARBER, MANNY. "Jackson Pollock," *New Republic,* June 25, 1945, pp. 871–72.

62. FITZSIMMONS, JAMES. [Reviews.] *Art Digest,* XXVI, December 15, 1951, p. 19; XXVII, November 15, 1952, p. 17. – *Arts & Architecture,* LXXI, March 1954, pp. 7f.

FOLDS, THOMAS M., *see* No. 10.
FRAMPTON, KENNETH, *see* No. 11.

63. FRANKENSTEIN, ALFRED. [Review.] *San Francisco Chronicle,* August 12, 1945.

64. FREMANTLE, CHRISTOPHER E. "New York Commentary," *Studio* (London), CXLVII, June 1954, pp. 184f.

65. FRIED, MICHAEL. "Jackson Pollock," *Artforum,* IV, September 1965, pp. 14–17.

A selection from the introductory essay in HARVARD UNIVERSITY, FOGG ART MUSEUM. *Three American Painters: Kenneth Noland, Jules Olitski, Frank Stella.* April 21–May 30, 1965.

66. ———. [Review.] *Art International,* VIII, April 1964, pp. 57–58.

67. FRIEDMAN, B. H. "Profile: Jackson Pollock," *Art in America,* XLIII, December 1955, pp. 49ff.

68. FRIGERIO, SIMONE. "Zürich. Pollock," *Aujourd'hui* (Paris), No. 34, December 1961, pp. 60–61.

69. GALTIERI, GIOVANNI. "Il Presley della pittura," *Avanti* (Rome), March 22, 1958.

70. GENAUER, EMILY. [Review.] *New York World-Telegram,* February 7, 1949.

71. ———. [Review.] *New York Herald-Tribune,* May 28, 1950; February 7, 1954.

72. ———. "Jackson Pollock's Endless Search," *New York Herald-Tribune: New York,* January 19, 1964, p. 29.

73. ———. [Review.] *World Journal Tribune,* April 4, 1967.

74. GERNER, KLAUS. "Vom Chaos bis zu Pollock," *Der Tag,* September 5, 1958.

75. GLASER, BRUCE. "Jackson Pollock. An Interview with Lee Krasner," *Arts Magazine,* XLI, April 1967, pp. 36–38.

76. GOODNOUGH, ROBERT. "Pollock Paints a Picture," *Art News,* L, May 1951, pp. 38ff.

77. ———. [Reviews.] *Art News,* XLIX, December 1950, p. 47; LI, December 1952, pp. 42–43.

GRAY, CLEVE, *see* No. 146.

78. GRAHAM, HUGH. "Trails of the Unconscious," *Spectator* (London), CCVI, June 2, 1961, p. 797.

79. GREENBERG, CLEMENT. [Reviews.] *Nation,* November 27, 1943, p. 621; April 7, 1945, p. 397; April 13, 1946, p. 445; December 28, 1946, p. 768; February 1, 1947, pp. 137, 139; January 24, 1948, p. 108; February 19, 1949, p. 221.

80. ———. "The Present Prospects of American Painting and Sculpture," *Horizon* (London), No. 93–94, October 1947, pp. 20–30.

81. ———. "Art Chronicle: Feeling Is All," *Partisan Review,* XIX, January-February 1952, p. 102.

82. ———. "Jackson Pollock's New Style," *Harper's Bazaar,* LXXXV, February 1952, p. 174.

83. ———. " 'American-Type' Painting," *Partisan Review,* XXII, Spring 1955, pp. 186–87. Reprinted in somewhat revised form in his *Art and Culture,* Boston: Beacon Press, 1961.

84. ———. "Jackson Pollock," *Evergreen Review,* I, 1957, pp. 95–96.

85. ———. "The Jackson Pollock Market Soars," *New York Times Magazine,* April 16, 1961, pp. 42ff.

Issue of April 30, 1961 contains letters to the editor.

86. ———. "America Takes the Lead, 1945–1965," *Art in America,* LIII, August/September 1965, p. 108.

87. ———. "Jackson Pollock: 'Inspiration, Vision, Intuitive Decision,' " *Vogue,* CXLIX, April 1, 1967, pp. 160–61.

88. GROHMANN, WILL. [Review.] *Tagesspiegel* (Berlin), September 7, 1958.

89. GRUEN, JOHN. "A Turbulent Life with Jackson Pollock," *New York—World Journal Tribune,* March 26, 1967, pp. 14–15.

90. GUÉGUEN, PIERRE. "Pollock et la nouvelle peinture américaine," *Aujourd'hui* (Paris), No. 21, March-April 1959, pp. 30–33.

91. "Handful of Fire," *Time,* LIV, December 26, 1949, p. 26.

92. HARRISON, STANLEY. "*Lavender Mist* by Jackson Pollock. A Critique." Typescript in the Library, The Museum of Modern Art, New York, n.d. Pp. 7.

93. "The Hero-Figure of Action-Painting," *Times* (London), November 11, 1958.

94. H[ESS], T[HOMAS] B. "Jackson Pollock 1912–1956," *Art News,* LV, September 1956, pp. 44–45.

95. ———. [Reviews.] *Art News,* LIII, March 1954, pp. 40–41; LV, February 1957, pp. 8–9.

96. HESS, THOMAS B. "Pollock: The Art of a Myth," *Art News,* LXII, January 1964, pp. 39ff.

97. HODGSON, SIMON. "Neurasthenic Dazzle," *Spectator* (London), CCI, November 21, 1958, pp. 688–89.

98. HOFFMAN, EDITH. "New York," *Burlington Magazine,* XCIX, February 1957, p. 68.

99. HORN, AXEL. "Jackson Pollock: The Hollow and the Bump," *Carleton Miscellany* (Northfield, Minn.), VII, Summer 1966, pp. 80–87.

100. "How They Got That Way," *Time,* LXXIX, April 13, 1962, pp. 94–99.

101. HUNTER, SAM. "Abstract Expressionism Then —and Now," *Canadian Art,* XXI, September/October 1964, pp. 266–68.

102. ——. [Review.] *New York Times,* January 30, 1949.
——, *see* Nos. 204, 205.

103. IMBOURG, PIERRE. "Avez-vous vu Pollock?" *Journal de l'Amateur d'Art* (Paris), XIII, January 25, 1959, p. 3.

104. "Jackson Pollock: An Artists' Symposium, Part 1," *Art News,* LXVI, April 1967, pp. 29ff.
Statements by James Brooks, Adolph Gottlieb, Al Held, Allan Kaprow, Alex Katz, Elaine de Kooning, Robert Motherwell, Barnett Newman, Philip Pavia, Larry Rivers.

105. "Jackson Pollock: An Artists' Symposium, Part 2," *ibid.,* May 1967, pp. 27ff.
Statements by Al Brunelle, Jane Freilicher, David Lee, Joan Mitchell, Kenneth Noland, David Novros, Claes Oldenburg, George Segal.

106. "Jackson Pollock: Is He the Greatest Living Painter in the United States?" *Life,* XXVII, August 8, 1949, pp. 42ff.

107. JEWELL, EDWARD ALDEN. [Review.] *New York Times,* November 14, 1943.

107a. JEWETT, ELEANOR. [Review.] *Chicago Daily Tribune,* March 6, 1945.

108. JUDD, DON. "Jackson Pollock," *Arts,* XLI, April 1967, pp. 32–35.

109. KAPROW, ALLAN. "The Legacy of Jackson Pollock," *Art News,* LVII, October 1958, pp. 24–26.
Letter from Irving H. Sandler, *ibid.,* December 1958; reply by Kaprow, *ibid.,* February 1959.

110. ——. "Impurity," *Art News,* LXI, January 1963, pp. 53–54.

111. KARP, IVAN C. "In Memoriam: The Ecstasy and Tragedy of Jackson Pollock, Artist," *Village Voice* (New York), September 26, 1956.

112. K[OONING], E[LAINE DE]. [Review.] *Art News,* XLVIII, March 1949, p. 44.

113. KOZLOFF, MAX. [Review.] *Nation,* February 10, 1964, pp. 151–52.

114. ——. "The Critical Reception of Abstract-Expressionism," *Arts,* XL, December 1965, pp. 27–33.
Article based on a lecture given at the Los Angeles County Museum of Art August 1965 in connection with the exhibition *New York School;* see No. 215.

115. KRAMER, HILTON. "Month in Review," *Arts,* XXXI, February 1957, pp. 46–48.

116. ——. "Jackson Pollock and Nicolas de Staël. Two Painters and Their Myths," *Arts Yearbook,* No. 3, 1959, pp. 53–60.

117. ——. [Reviews.] *New York Times,* April 5, 1967; April 9, 1967.

118. K[RASNE], B[ELLE]. [Review.] *Art Digest,* XXV, December 1, 1950, p. 16.

119. KROLL, JACK. "A Magic Life," *Newsweek,* April 17, 1967, p. 96.

120. LAMBERT, JEAN-CLARENCE. "Observations sur Jackson Pollock et la nouvelle peinture américaine," *Cahiers du Musée de Poche,* No. 2, June 1959, pp. 108–12.

121. LA MOTTE, MANFRED DE. "Jackson Pollock in Kunstverein Düsseldorf," *Kunstwerk,* XV, October 1961.

121a. L[ANE], J[AMES]. [Review.] *Art News,* XL, January 15–31, 1942, p. 29.

122. L[ANSFORD], A[LONZO]. "Automatic Pollock," *Art Digest,* XXII, January 15, 1948, p. 19.

123. LAVIN, IRVING. "Abstraction in Modern Painting: A Comparison," *Metropolitan Museum of Art Bulletin,* XIX, February 1961, pp. 166–71.
Includes an analysis of *Autumn Rhythm.*

124. "A Life Round Table on Modern Art," *Life,* XXV, October 11, 1948, pp. 56–70, 75–79.

125. LOUCHHEIM, ALINE B. [Review.] *New York Times,* September 10, 1950.

126. LAWS, FREDERICK. "Jackson Pollock in Perspective. Much More than 'Drool,'" *Manchester Guardian,* November 10, 1958.

127. L[OWENGRUND], M[ARGARET]. "Pollock Hieroglyphics," *Art Digest,* XXIII, February 1, 1949, pp. 19–20.

128. McBRIDE, HENRY. "Not Bad for These Times," *Art News,* L, April 1951, pp. 38–39.

129. ——. [Review.] *New York Sun,* December 23, 1949.

130. McCLURE, MIKE. "Ode to Jackson Pollock," *Evergreen Review,* II, Autumn 1958, pp. 124–26.

131. MACMULLEN, ROY. "L'Ecole de New York: Des concurrents dangereux," *Connaissance des Arts,* No. 115, September 1961, pp. 30–37.

132. M[ARCHIORI], G[IUSEPPE]. "Pollock," *XXe Siècle,* N.S. No. 8, January 1957, p. 86.
Also in Italian in *Notiziario,* No. 5, April 1958, pp. 6–8.

133. MELVILLE, ROBERT. [Reviews.] *Architectural Review,* CXIX, May 1956, pp. 267–68; CXXV, February 1959, p. 139; CXXX, August 1961, pp. 130–31. – *Arts,* XXXIII, January 1959, p. 16.

134. MENNA, FILIBERTO. "'L'Astrattismo romantico' di Jackson Pollock," *Commentari* (Rome), IX, July–September 1958, pp. 206–15.

135. MICACCHI, DARIO. "Il Deserto dell'impotenza nella pittura di Pollock," *L'Unità* (Rome), March 12, 1958.

136. MICHELSON, ANNETTE. "Paris," *Arts,* XXXIII, June 1959, pp. 17–18.
Review of and summary of reactions to the two exhibitions, organized under the auspices of the International Council at The Museum of Modern Art, shown simultaneously in Paris, *Jackson Pollock 1912–1956* and *The New American Painting.* – See Nos. 206, 206a.

137. MIDDLETON, MICHAEL. "Pollock," *Motif* (London), No. 2, February 1959, pp. 80–81.

138. MOCK, JEAN YVES. "Pollock at the Whitechapel Gallery," *Apollo*, LXVIII, December 1958, p. 221.

139. MOTHERWELL, ROBERT. "Painters' Objects," *Partisan Review*, XI, Winter 1944, pp. 93–97.

140. NAMUTH, HANS. "Jackson Pollock," *Portfolio. The Annual of the Graphic Arts* (Cincinnati), 1951, 6 pp.

141. NEWTON, ERIC. "Jackson Pollock at the Whitechapel Gallery," *Time and Tide* (London), XXXIX, November 15, 1958, p. 1371.

142. NUGENT, JOSEPH F. "Some Thoughts on Pollock," *New Bulletin* (Staten Island Institute of Arts and Sciences), XI, April 1962, pp. 94–95.

143. O'CONNOR, FRANCIS V. "Growth Out of Need," *Report*, I, February 1964, pp. 27–28.

144. ———. "The Genesis of Jackson Pollock: 1912 to 1943," *Artforum*, V, May 1967, pp. 16–23.

144a. O'HARA, FRANK. "Jackson Pollock 1912–1956," in SELZ, PETER. *New Images of Man*. New York: The Museum of Modern Art, 1959, pp. 123–28.

145. PLATSCHEK, HANS. "Der Fall Pollock," *Baukunst und Werkform*, XIII, January 1960, pp. 43–44.

146. PLESSIX, FRANCINE DU and GRAY, CLEVE. "Who Was Jackson Pollock?" *Art in America*, May–June 1967, pp. 48–59.
Interviews with Alfonso Ossorio, Betty Parsons, Lee Krasner Pollock, Anthony Smith.

147. "Pollock Revisited," *Time*, LXXXIX, April 14, 1967, p. 85.

148. P[ORTER], F[AIRFIELD]. [Review.] *Art News*, L, December 1951, p. 48.

149. PRESTON, STUART. [Reviews.] *New York Times*, November 27, 1949; December 4, 1955.

150. RAYNOR, VIVIEN. "Jackson Pollock in Retrospect—'He Broke the Ice,'" *New York Times Magazine*, April 2, 1967, pp. 50ff.

151. READ, HERBERT. "The Limits of Painting," *Studio* (London), CLXVII, January 1964, pp. 3–4.

152. RESTANY, PIERRE. "L'Art aux Etats-Unis: Jackson Pollock, l'éclabousseur," *Prisme des Arts* (Paris), No. 15, p. 19.

153. REXROTH, KENNETH. "Americans Seen Abroad," *Art News*, LVIII, June 1959, pp. 30ff.

154. RILEY, MAUDE. [Reviews.] *Art Digest*, XVIII, November 15, 1943, p. 18; XIX, April 1, 1945, p. 59.

155. R[OBINSON], A[MY]. [Review.] *Art News*, XLVIII, December 1949, p. 43.

156. ROSE, BARBARA. "New York Letter," *Art International*, VIII, April 1964, p. 52.

157. ROSENBERG, HAROLD. [Review.] *New Yorker*, XLIII, May 6, 1967, pp. 162–71.
———, see Nos. 11, 161.

158. ROSENBLUM, ROBERT. "The Abstract Sublime," *Art News*, LIX, February 1961, p. 41.

159. RUBIN, WILLIAM. "Letter from New York," *Art International*, II, December 1958–January 1959, pp. 27–28.

160. ———. "Notes on Masson and Pollock," *Arts*, XXXIV, November 1959, pp. 36–43; December 1959, p. 9.

161. ———. "Jackson Pollock and the Modern Tradition," *Artforum*, V, February 1967, pp. 14–22; March 1967, pp. 28–37; April 1967, pp. 18–31; May 1967, pp. 28–33.
The April and May issues contain correspondence between Harold Rosenberg and William Rubin.

162. RUSSELL, JOHN. "Yankee Doodles," *Sunday Times* (London), January 8, 1956.

163. ———. "Pollock in Panorama," *Sunday Times* (London), November 9, 1958.

164. ———. "The 'New American Painting' Captures Europe," *Horizon* (London), XI, November 1959, pp. 32–41.

165. RUSSO, GIOVANNI. "Una Mostra di Pollock a Roma provoca discordie tra i pittori di sinistra," *Corriere d'Informazione* (Milan), March 26/27, 1958.
SANDLER, IRVING H., see No. 109.

166. SAWYER, KENNETH B. "Jackson Pollock. 1912–1956," *Cimaise* (Paris), Ser. 4, No. 2, November–December 1956, pp. 22–23.
English tr. p. 10.

167. SCHAPIRO, MEYER. "The Younger American Painters of Today," *Listener* (London), LV, January 26, 1956, pp. 146–47.
Talk delivered on the BBC on the occasion of the exhibition *Modern Art in the United States* shown at the Tate Gallery.

168. SCHNEIDER, PIERRE. "Paris," *Art News*, LVIII, March 1959, p. 47.
Review of the two exhibitions, organized under the auspices of the International Council at The Museum of Modern Art, shown simultaneously in Paris, *Jackson Pollock 1912–1956* and *The New American Painting.* – See Nos. 206, 206a.

169. SCHOENENBERGER, GUALTIERO. "Jackson Pollock," *Art International*, V, December 1961, pp. 49–50.
In French.

170. S[CHUYLER], J[AMES]. [Reviews.] *Art News*, LVI, December 1957, p. 10; LVII, December 1958, p. 12.

171. SEIBERLING, DOROTHY. "Baffling U.S. Art: What It Is About," *Life*, XLVII, November 9, 1959, pp. 68–80; November 16, 1959, pp. 74–86.
A two-part series on Abstract Expressionism in the United States; part 1 is devoted primarily to Pollock.

172. SEIXAS, FRANK A. "Jackson Pollock. An Appreciation," *Art Gallery*, VII, October 1963, pp. 11–13.

173. SMITH, RICHARD. "Jackson Pollock 1912–1956," *Art News and Review* (London), X, November 22, 1958, p. 5.

174. STEINBERG, LEO. "Month in Review," *Arts,* XXX, December 1955, pp. 43–44.

175. STRAUSS, MICHEL. "London," *Burlington Magazine,* CIII, July 1961, pp. 327f.

176. SUTTON, DENYS. "Modern Art in the United States," *Country Life* (London), CXIX, January 19, 1956, pp. 102–3.

177. ——. "Jackson Pollock," *Financial Times* (London), November 25, 1958, p. 13.

178. SYLVESTER, DAVID. [Review.] *Nation,* September 9, 1950, p. 232.

179. TAYLOR, BASIL. "Modern American Painting," *Spectator* (London), No. 6656, January 20, 1956, p. 80.

180. THARRATS, J[OAN] J[OSEP]. "Artistas de hoy: Jackson Pollock," *Revista* (Barcelona), February 2, 1957.

181. TILLIM, SIDNEY. "Jackson Pollock. A Critical Evaluation," *College Art Journal,* XVI, Spring 1957, pp. 242–43.

182. ——. [Reviews.] *Arts,* XXXIII, December 1958, p. 53; XXXVIII, March 1964, pp. 55–59.

182a. TYLER, PARKER. "Nature and Madness Among the Younger Painters," *View* (New York), V, May 1945, pp. 30–31.

183. ——. "Jackson Pollock: The Infinite Labyrinth," *Magazine of Art,* XLIII, March 1950, pp. 92–93.

184. ——. [Review.] *Art News,* LIV, December 1955, p. 53.

185. ——. "Hopper/Pollock. The Loneliness of the Crowd and the Loneliness of the Universe: An Antiphonal," *Art News Annual,* XXVI, 1957, pp. 86–107.

——, see No. 11.

185a. [Unsigned review.] *The Compass* (New York), December 3, 1950.

186. VALLIERE, JAMES T. "The El Greco Influence on Jackson Pollock's Early Works," *Art Journal,* XXIV, Fall 1964, pp. 6–9.

187. VALSECCHI, MARCO. "Il Vulcanico Pollock," *Tempo* (Milan), n.d.

188. VAN DEN BERG, FREEK. [Review.] *Het Vrije Volk* (Amsterdam), June 21, 1958.

189. VENTURI, LIONELLO. "La Mostra di Pollock," *L'Espresso* (Rome), March 23, 1958.

190. VENTUROLI, MARCELLO. "Jackson Pollock e gli astrattisti italiani," *Paese Sera* (Rome), March 13/14, 1958.

191. WALLIS, NEVILE. "Heroes of the Day," *Observer* (London), November 9, 1958.

192. WASHBURN, GORDON BAILEY. "Three Gifts to the Gallery," *Carnegie Magazine,* XXVII, December 1953, pp. 337–38.

193. WHITTET, G. S. "London Commentary," *Studio* (London), CLVII, February 1959, p. 58.

194. "The Wild Ones," *Time,* LXVII, February 20, 1956, pp. 70–75.

195. WILLING, VICTOR. "Thoughts After a Car Crash," *Encounter,* VII, October 1956, pp. 66–68.

196. WOLF, BEN. [Reviews.] *Art Digest,* XX, April 15, 1946, p. 16; XXI, January 15, 1947, p. 21.

197. "Words," *Time,* LIII, February 7, 1949, p. 51.

197a. "The Year's Best: 1950," *Art News,* XLIX, January 1951, pp. 42–43, 58–59.

197b. "The Year's Best: 1952," *Art News,* LI, January 1953, pp. 42–43.

EXHIBITION CATALOGUES
(arranged chronologically)

198. NEW YORK, ART OF THIS CENTURY. *Jackson Pollock.* November 9–27, 1943. Pp. 4.
Introduction by James Johnson Sweeney. Reprinted in catalogue of Pollock exhibition at the Arts Club of Chicago, March 5–31, 1945; in *It Is* (New York), No. 4, Autumn 1959, p. 56.

199. NEW YORK, ART OF THIS CENTURY. *Jackson Pollock.* January 14–February 1, 1947. Pp. 4. Introduction by [W.] N. M. Davis.

200. VENICE, ALA NAPOLEONICA (MUSEO CORRER). *Jackson Pollock.* July 22–August 12/15, 1950. Pp. 8.
Two catalogues printed: the first gives Le Tre Mani as sponsors, contains introductory remarks by Peggy Guggenheim and an essay, " 'Guazzabugli' di Jackson Pollock," by Bruno Alfieri; the second contains only the remarks by Peggy Guggenheim.

201. NEW YORK, BETTY PARSONS GALLERY. *Jackson Pollock.* November 26–December 15, 1951. Pp. 18.
Introduction by Alfonso Ossorio. Reprinted (in French) in No. 202; with slight alterations in NEW YORK, THE MUSEUM OF MODERN ART, *15 Americans,* April 9–July 27, 1952; in NEW YORK, THE MUSEUM OF MODERN ART, *The New American Painting,* May 28–September 8, 1959.

202. PARIS, STUDIO PAUL FACCHETTI. *Jackson Pollock.* March 7–31, 1952. Pp. 8.
Essays by Michel Tapié, "Jackson Pollock avec nous," and Alfonso Ossorio, "Mon ami Pollock" (*see* No. 201).

202a. NEW YORK, THE MUSEUM OF MODERN ART. *15 Americans.* April 9–July 27, 1952. 8 works by Pollock.
Essay on Pollock by Alfonso Ossorio, *see* No. 201.

203. NEW YORK, SIDNEY JANIS GALLERY. *15 Years of Jackson Pollock.* November 28–December 31, 1955. Pp. 16.

204. NEW YORK, THE MUSEUM OF MODERN ART. *Jackson Pollock.* December 19, 1956–February 3, 1957. Pp. 36. (The Museum of Modern Art Bulletin, XXIV, No. 2, 1956–57.)
Text by Sam Hunter. Reprinted in English and Portuguese in No. 205; in English and other languages in No. 206.

205. NEW YORK, THE INTERNATIONAL COUNCIL AT THE MUSEUM OF MODERN ART. *Pollock* (Reprecentação dos Estados Unidos à IV Bienal do Museu de arte moderna de São Paulo). September 22–December 31, 1957. Pp. 36.

Text by Sam Hunter, in English and Portuguese, adapted from No. 204.

206. NEW YORK, THE INTERNATIONAL COUNCIL AT THE MUSEUM OF MODERN ART. *Jackson Pollock 1912–1956.* March 1, 1958–February 15, 1959.

Translations of text by Sam Hunter, adapted from No. 204, in separate catalogues published in each city: ROME, GALLERIA NAZIONALE D'ARTE MODERNA, March 1–30, 1958; BASEL, KUNSTHALLE, April 19–May 26, 1958; AMSTERDAM, STEDELIJK MUSEUM, June 6–July 7, 1958; HAMBURG, KUNSTVEREIN, July 19–August 17, 1958 (joint catalogue with Basel Kunsthalle); BERLIN, HOCHSCHULE FÜR BILDENDE KÜNSTE, September 1–October 1, 1958; LONDON, WHITECHAPEL ART GALLERY, November 4–December 14, 1958; PARIS, MUSÉE NATIONAL D'ART MODERNE, January 16–February 15, 1959 (shown simultaneously with *The New American Painting;* joint catalogue, *Jackson Pollock et La nouvelle peinture américaine*).

206a. NEW YORK, THE MUSEUM OF MODERN ART. *The New American Painting.* May 28–September 8, 1959. Pp. 96. 4 works by Pollock.

Exhibition, selected by Dorothy C. Miller, as shown in eight European cities April 1958–March 1959 under the auspices of the International Program of The Museum of Modern Art. Catalogue is a reprint of the one used for the showing at the Tate Gallery, London, February–March 1959, with the addition of colorplates and a selection of critical response that appeared in European publications.

207. LONDON, MARLBOROUGH FINE ART LTD. *Jackson Pollock. Paintings, Drawings, and Watercolors from the Collection of Lee Krasner Pollock.* June 1961. Pp. 64.

Introduction and catalogue notes by Lawrence Alloway. Reprinted in various translations in Nos. 208–210; in *Paletten* (Stockholm), XXII, 1961, pp. 82–85.

208. DÜSSELDORF, KUNSTVEREIN FÜR DIE RHEINLÄNDE UND WESTFALEN. KUNSTHALLE. *Jackson Pollock.* September 5–October 8, 1961. Pp. 55.

Preface by Karl-Heinz Hering. Introduction and catalogue notes by Lawrence Alloway, German translation of No. 207.

209. ZURICH, KUNSTHAUS. *Jackson Pollock.* October 24–November 29, 1961. Pp. 59.

Preface by Eduard Hüttinger. Introduction and catalogue notes by Lawrence Alloway, German translation of No. 207.

210. ROME, MARLBOROUGH GALLERIA D'ARTE. *Jackson Pollock.* October–November, 1962. Pp. 12.

Introduction by Lawrence Alloway, Italian translation of No. 207. – Same exhibition shown in Milan, Toninelli Arte Moderna, November–December 1962, for which a separate catalogue was published.

211. STOCKHOLM, MODERNA MUSEET. *Jackson Pollock.* February–April 1963. Pp. 34.

Introduction by K. G. Hultén.

212. NEW YORK, MARLBOROUGH–GERSON GALLERY. *Jackson Pollock.* January–February 1964. Pp. 64.

Brief introduction by Bryan Robertson, excerpt from No. 11.

213. HARVARD UNIVERSITY, FOGG ART MUSEUM. *Within the Easel Convention: Sources of Abstract-Expressionism.* May 7–June 7, 1964. Pp. 46. 3 works by Pollock.

Text by Ann Gabhart, Frieda Grayzel, Rosalind Krauss. Analysis of Pollock's works by Ann Gabhart.

214. LONDON, TATE GALLERY. *The Peggy Guggenheim Collection.* December 31, 1964–March 7, 1965. Pp. 99. 11 works by Pollock.

Preface by Herbert Read. Introduction by Peggy Guggenheim. Catalogue notes by Ronald Alley.

215. LOS ANGELES COUNTY MUSEUM OF ART. *New York School. The First Generation. Paintings of the 1940s and 1950s.* July 16–August 1, 1965. Pp. 232. 8 works by Pollock.

Edited by Maurice Tuchman.

216. COLLEGE PARK, UNIVERSITY OF MARYLAND ART GALLERY. *Federal Art Patronage 1933 to 1943.* April 6–May 13, 1966. Pp. 60. 2 works by Pollock.

Text by Francis V. O'Connor.

FILM

217. *Jackson Pollock.* Produced by Hans Namuth and Paul Falkenberg. Music by Morton Feldman. Narration by Jackson Pollock. 1951.

10 minutes. 16 mm. Color. Sound. – Distributed by Film Images, 220 West 42nd Street, New York City.

Index

Page numbers printed in italics refer to illustrations. Catalogue numbers are given in parentheses for works in the exhibition.